Predictive Analytics
Complete Self-Assessment Guide

The guidance in this Self-Assessment is based on Predictive Analytics best practices and standards in business process architecture, design and quality management. The guidance is also based on the professional judgment of the individual collaborators listed in the Acknowledgments.

Notice of rights

Trademarks

Table of Contents

About The Art of Service

The Art of Service, Business Process Architects since 2000, is dedicated to helping stakeholders achieve excellence.

Defining, designing, creating, and implementing a process to solve a stakeholders challenge or meet an objective is the most valuable role... In EVERY group, company, organization and department.

Unless you're talking a one-time, single-use project, there should be a process. Whether that process is managed and implemented by humans, AI, or a combination of the two, it needs to be designed by someone with a complex enough perspective to ask the right questions.

Someone capable of asking the right questions and step back and say, 'What are we really trying to accomplish here? And is there a different way to look at it?'

With The Art of Service's Standard Requirements Self-Assessments, we empower people who can do just that — whether their title is marketer, entrepreneur, manager, salesperson, consultant, Business Process Manager, executive assistant, IT Manager, CIO etc... —they are the people who rule the future. They are people who watch the process as it happens, and ask the right questions to make the process work better.

Contact us when you need any support with this Self-Assessment and any help with templates, blue-prints and examples of standard documents you might need:

http://theartofservice.com
service@theartofservice.com

Acknowledgments

This checklist was developed under the auspices of The Art of Service, chaired by Gerardus Blokdyk.

Representatives from several client companies participated in the preparation of this Self-Assessment.

In addition, we are thankful for the design and printing services provided.

Included Resources - how to access

Included with your purchase of the book is the Predictive Analytics Self-Assessment Spreadsheet Dashboard which contains all questions and Self-Assessment areas and auto-generates insights, graphs, and project RACI planning - all with examples to get you started right away.

How? Simply send an email to
access@theartofservice.com
with this books' title in the subject to get the Predictive Analytics Self Assessment Tool right away.

You will receive the following contents with New and Updated specific criteria:

- The latest quick edition of the book in PDF

- The latest complete edition of the book in PDF, which criteria correspond to the criteria in...

- The Self-Assessment Excel Dashboard, and...

- Example pre-filled Self-Assessment Excel Dashboard to get familiar with results generation

- In-depth specific Checklists covering the topic

- Project management checklists and templates to assist with implementation

INCLUDES LIFETIME SELF ASSESSMENT UPDATES

Every self assessment comes with Lifetime Updates and Lifetime Free Updated Books. Lifetime Updates is an industry-first feature which allows you to receive verified self assessment updates, ensuring you always have the most accurate information at your fingertips.

Get it now- you will be glad you did - do it now, before you forget.

Send an email to **access@theartofservice.com** with this books' title in the subject to get the Predictive Analytics Self Assessment Tool right away.

Your feedback is invaluable to us

If you recently bought this book, we would love to hear from you! You can do this by writing a review on amazon (or the online store where you purchased this book) about your last purchase! As part of our continual service improvement process, we love to hear real client experiences and feedback.

How does it work?
To post a review on Amazon, just log in to your account and click on the Create Your Own Review button (under Customer Reviews) of the relevant product page. You can find examples of product reviews in Amazon. If you purchased from another online store, simply follow their procedures.

What happens when I submit my review?
Once you have submitted your review, send us an email at review@theartofservice.com with the link to your review so we can properly thank you for your feedback.

Purpose of this Self-Assessment

This Self-Assessment has been developed to improve understanding of the requirements and elements of Predictive Analytics, based on best practices and standards in business process architecture, design and quality management.

It is designed to allow for a rapid Self-Assessment to determine how closely existing management practices and procedures correspond to the elements of the Self-Assessment.

The criteria of requirements and elements of Predictive Analytics have been rephrased in the format of a Self-Assessment questionnaire, with a seven-criterion scoring system, as explained in this document.

In this format, even with limited background knowledge of

Predictive Analytics, a manager can quickly review existing operations to determine how they measure up to the standards. This in turn can serve as the starting point of a 'gap analysis' to identify management tools or system elements that might usefully be implemented in the organization to help improve overall performance.

How to use the Self-Assessment

On the following pages are a series of questions to identify to what extent your Predictive Analytics initiative is complete in comparison to the requirements set in standards.

To facilitate answering the questions, there is a space in front of each question to enter a score on a scale of '1' to '5'.

1 Strongly Disagree

2 Disagree

3 Neutral

4 Agree

5 Strongly Agree

Read the question and rate it with the following in front of mind:

**'In my belief,
the answer to this question is clearly defined'.**

There are two ways in which you can choose to interpret this statement;
1. how aware are you that the answer to the question is clearly defined
2. for more in-depth analysis you can choose to gather

evidence and confirm the answer to the question. This obviously will take more time, most Self-Assessment users opt for the first way to interpret the question and dig deeper later on based on the outcome of the overall Self-Assessment.

A score of '1' would mean that the answer is not clear at all, where a '5' would mean the answer is crystal clear and defined. Leave emtpy when the question is not applicable or you don't want to answer it, you can skip it without affecting your score. Write your score in the space provided.

After you have responded to all the appropriate statements in each section, compute your average score for that section, using the formula provided, and round to the nearest tenth. Then transfer to the corresponding spoke in the Predictive Analytics Scorecard on the second next page of the Self-Assessment.

Your completed Predictive Analytics Scorecard will give you a clear presentation of which Predictive Analytics areas need attention.

Predictive Analytics Scorecard Example

Example of how the finalized Scorecard can look like:

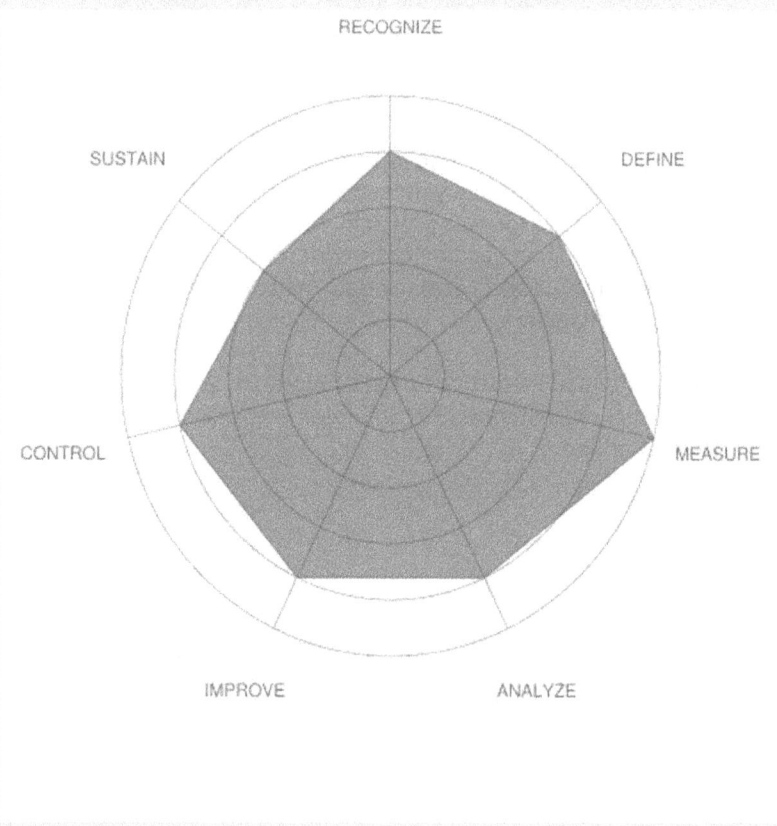

Predictive Analytics Scorecard

Your Scores:

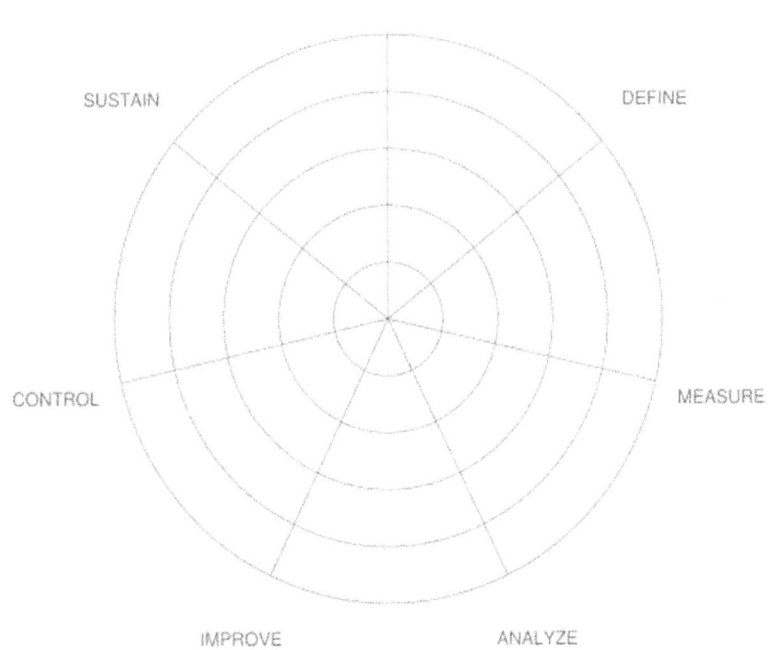

BEGINNING OF THE SELF-ASSESSMENT:

CRITERION #1: RECOGNIZE

INTENT: Be aware of the need for change. Recognize that there is an unfavorable variation, problem or symptom.

In my belief, the answer to this question is clearly defined:

5 Strongly Agree

4 Agree

3 Neutral

2 Disagree

1 Strongly Disagree

1. Are your goals realistic? Do you need to redefine your problem? Perhaps the problem has changed or maybe you have reached your goal and need to set a new one?
<--- Score

2. How are you going to measure success?
<--- Score

3. What extra resources will you need?
<--- Score

4. Who had the original idea?
<--- Score

5. What training and capacity building actions are needed to implement proposed reforms?
<--- Score

6. Are there any revenue recognition issues?
<--- Score

7. For your Predictive Analytics project, identify and describe the business environment, is there more than one layer to the business environment?
<--- Score

8. How do you take a forward-looking perspective in identifying Predictive Analytics research related to market response and models?
<--- Score

9. Are you dealing with any of the same issues today as yesterday? What can you do about this?
<--- Score

10. What is the smallest subset of the problem you can usefully solve?
<--- Score

11. How much are sponsors, customers, partners, stakeholders involved in Predictive Analytics? In other words, what are the risks, if Predictive Analytics does not deliver successfully?
<--- Score

12. Are controls defined to recognize and contain problems?

<--- Score

13. What kind of support is needed?

<--- Score

14. Do you know what you need to know about Predictive Analytics?

<--- Score

15. Does your organization need more Predictive Analytics education?

<--- Score

16. Who else hopes to benefit from it?

<--- Score

17. What needs to be done?

<--- Score

18. Does Predictive Analytics create potential expectations in other areas that need to be recognized and considered?

<--- Score

19. Does aggregation exceed permissible need to know about an individual?

<--- Score

20. Do you need different information or graphics?

<--- Score

21. What do you need to start doing?

<--- Score

22. What is the experience level and education of the staff who will need to be trained?
<--- Score

23. Are there any specific expectations or concerns about the Predictive Analytics team, Predictive Analytics itself?
<--- Score

24. Are employees recognized or rewarded for performance that demonstrates the highest levels of integrity?
<--- Score

25. How are the Predictive Analytics's objectives aligned to the organization's overall business strategy?
<--- Score

26. Who needs to know about Predictive Analytics?
<--- Score

27. To what extent would your organization benefit from being recognized as a award recipient?
<--- Score

28. What should be considered when identifying available resources, constraints, and deadlines?
<--- Score

29. Will Predictive Analytics deliverables need to be tested and, if so, by whom?
<--- Score

30. What vendors make products that address the

Predictive Analytics needs?
<--- Score

31. What would happen if Predictive Analytics weren't done?
<--- Score

32. What tools and technologies are needed for a custom Predictive Analytics project?
<--- Score

33. How does it fit into your organizational needs and tasks?
<--- Score

34. Are problem definition and motivation clearly presented?
<--- Score

35. Think about the people you identified for your Predictive Analytics project and the project responsibilities you would assign to them. what kind of training do you think they would need to perform these responsibilities effectively?
<--- Score

36. What are the minority interests and what amount of minority interests can be recognized?
<--- Score

37. Who are your key stakeholders who need to sign off?
<--- Score

38. How can auditing be a preventative security measure?

<--- Score

39. What problems are you facing and how do you consider Predictive Analytics will circumvent those obstacles?
<--- Score

40. How do you assess your Predictive Analytics workforce capability and capacity needs, including skills, competencies, and staffing levels?
<--- Score

41. Looking at each person individually – does every one have the qualities which are needed to work in this group?
<--- Score

42. Who defines the rules in relation to any given issue?
<--- Score

43. What are your needs in relation to Predictive Analytics skills, labor, equipment, and markets?
<--- Score

44. Who needs what information?
<--- Score

45. Will new equipment/products be required to facilitate Predictive Analytics delivery, for example is new software needed?
<--- Score

46. To what extent does each concerned units management team recognize Predictive Analytics as an effective investment?

<--- Score

47. What are the expected benefits of Predictive Analytics to the business?
<--- Score

48. What prevents you from making the changes you know will make you a more effective Predictive Analytics leader?
<--- Score

49. Consider your own Predictive Analytics project, what types of organizational problems do you think might be causing or affecting your problem, based on the work done so far?
<--- Score

50. Are there recognized Predictive Analytics problems?
<--- Score

51. Should you invest in industry-recognized qualications?
<--- Score

52. As a sponsor, customer or management, how important is it to meet goals, objectives?
<--- Score

53. What does Predictive Analytics success mean to the stakeholders?
<--- Score

54. What else needs to be measured?
<--- Score

55. Do you need to avoid or amend any Predictive Analytics activities?
<--- Score

56. Do you have/need 24-hour access to key personnel?
<--- Score

57. When a Predictive Analytics manager recognizes a problem, what options are available?
<--- Score

58. What are the timeframes required to resolve each of the issues/problems?
<--- Score

59. Will it solve real problems?
<--- Score

60. Are there Predictive Analytics problems defined?
<--- Score

61. How do you identify the kinds of information that you will need?
<--- Score

62. Is it clear when you think of the day ahead of you what activities and tasks you need to complete?
<--- Score

63. What are the business objectives to be achieved with Predictive Analytics?
<--- Score

64. Will a response program recognize when a crisis occurs and provide some level of response?

<--- Score

65. What information do users need?
<--- Score

66. What is the problem or issue?
<--- Score

67. What situation(s) led to this Predictive Analytics Self Assessment?
<--- Score

68. Can management personnel recognize the monetary benefit of Predictive Analytics?
<--- Score

Add up total points for this section:
_ _ _ _ _ = Total points for this section

Divided by: _ _ _ _ _ _ (number of statements answered) = _ _ _ _ _ _
Average score for this section

Transfer your score to the Predictive Analytics Index at the beginning of the Self-Assessment.

CRITERION #2: DEFINE:

INTENT: Formulate the business problem. Define the problem, needs and objectives.

In my belief, the answer to this question is clearly defined:

5 Strongly Agree

4 Agree

3 Neutral

2 Disagree

1 Strongly Disagree

1. How will the Predictive Analytics team and the organization measure complete success of Predictive Analytics?
<--- Score

2. How would you define the culture at your organization, how susceptible is it to Predictive Analytics changes?
<--- Score

3. What are the boundaries of the scope? What is in bounds and what is not? What is the start point? What is the stop point?
<--- Score

4. Are different versions of process maps needed to account for the different types of inputs?
<--- Score

5. How do you keep key subject matter experts in the loop?
<--- Score

6. Is Predictive Analytics linked to key business goals and objectives?
<--- Score

7. What was the context?
<--- Score

8. If substitutes have been appointed, have they been briefed on the Predictive Analytics goals and received regular communications as to the progress to date?
<--- Score

9. Is the team adequately staffed with the desired cross-functionality? If not, what additional resources are available to the team?
<--- Score

10. What are the Roles and Responsibilities for each team member and its leadership? Where is this documented?
<--- Score

11. What is the scope of the Predictive Analytics effort?
<--- Score

12. Is the Predictive Analytics scope complete and appropriately sized?
<--- Score

13. Are accountability and ownership for Predictive Analytics clearly defined?
<--- Score

14. What critical content must be communicated – who, what, when, where, and how?
<--- Score

15. How do you manage scope?
<--- Score

16. Has a team charter been developed and communicated?
<--- Score

17. Is there a Predictive Analytics management charter, including business case, problem and goal statements, scope, milestones, roles and responsibilities, communication plan?
<--- Score

18. Are approval levels defined for contracts and supplements to contracts?
<--- Score

19. In what way can you redefine the criteria of choice clients have in your category in your favor?
<--- Score

20. What is the scope?
<--- Score

21. What Predictive Analytics requirements should be gathered?
<--- Score

22. Who are the Predictive Analytics improvement team members, including Management Leads and Coaches?
<--- Score

23. What customer feedback methods were used to solicit their input?
<--- Score

24. How do you gather Predictive Analytics requirements?
<--- Score

25. Has the direction changed at all during the course of Predictive Analytics? If so, when did it change and why?
<--- Score

26. Has everyone on the team, including the team leaders, been properly trained?
<--- Score

27. Has your scope been defined?
<--- Score

28. Who defines (or who defined) the rules and roles?
<--- Score

29. Has a high-level 'as is' process map been completed, verified and validated?
<--- Score

30. How was the 'as is' process map developed, reviewed, verified and validated?
<--- Score

31. What are the rough order estimates on cost savings/opportunities that Predictive Analytics brings?
<--- Score

32. When was the Predictive Analytics start date?
<--- Score

33. What are the compelling business reasons for embarking on Predictive Analytics?
<--- Score

34. Is the team sponsored by a champion or business leader?
<--- Score

35. How do you hand over Predictive Analytics context?
<--- Score

36. Is the current 'as is' process being followed? If not, what are the discrepancies?
<--- Score

37. What sources do you use to gather information for a Predictive Analytics study?
<--- Score

38. What is in scope?
<--- Score

39. What key business process output measure(s) does Predictive Analytics leverage and how?
<--- Score

40. Are there different segments of customers?
<--- Score

41. Has anyone else (internal or external to the organization) attempted to solve this problem or a similar one before? If so, what knowledge can be leveraged from these previous efforts?
<--- Score

42. How do you think the partners involved in Predictive Analytics would have defined success?
<--- Score

43. Is Predictive Analytics required?
<--- Score

44. What constraints exist that might impact the team?
<--- Score

45. Is it clearly defined in and to your organization what you do?
<--- Score

46. At any point in time how many concurrent users will be required to access the application?
<--- Score

47. What happens if Predictive Analytics's scope

changes?
<--- Score

48. What are the dynamics of the communication plan?
<--- Score

49. How can the value of Predictive Analytics be defined?
<--- Score

50. Are team charters developed?
<--- Score

51. Are customers identified and high impact areas defined?
<--- Score

52. Has/have the customer(s) been identified?
<--- Score

53. Is there a completed SIPOC representation, describing the Suppliers, Inputs, Process, Outputs, and Customers?
<--- Score

54. What scope to assess?
<--- Score

55. What defines best in class?
<--- Score

56. Is the team formed and are team leaders (Coaches and Management Leads) assigned?
<--- Score

57. Does the scope remain the same?
<--- Score

58. Is the Predictive Analytics scope manageable?
<--- Score

59. Is the improvement team aware of the different versions of a process: what they think it is vs. what it actually is vs. what it should be vs. what it could be?
<--- Score

60. Are task requirements clearly defined?
<--- Score

61. Will team members regularly document their Predictive Analytics work?
<--- Score

62. Will team members perform Predictive Analytics work when assigned and in a timely fashion?
<--- Score

63. Is there a critical path to deliver Predictive Analytics results?
<--- Score

64. When are meeting minutes sent out? Who is on the distribution list?
<--- Score

65. Are customer(s) identified and segmented according to their different needs and requirements?
<--- Score

66. Scope of sensitive information?
<--- Score

67. Have the customer needs been translated into specific, measurable requirements? How?
<--- Score

68. Do the problem and goal statements meet the SMART criteria (specific, measurable, attainable, relevant, and time-bound)?
<--- Score

69. What are the tasks and definitions?
<--- Score

70. What are the most interesting cases of the use of crowdsourcing in a business model?
<--- Score

71. Is there regularly 100% attendance at the team meetings? If not, have appointed substitutes attended to preserve cross-functionality and full representation?
<--- Score

72. Has the improvement team collected the 'voice of the customer' (obtained feedback – qualitative and quantitative)?
<--- Score

73. Have specific policy objectives been defined?
<--- Score

74. Is scope creep really all bad news?
<--- Score

75. How and when will the baselines be defined?
<--- Score

76. What specifically is the problem? Where does it occur? When does it occur? What is its extent?
<--- Score

77. Is data collected and displayed to better understand customer(s) critical needs and requirements.
<--- Score

78. What are the record-keeping requirements of Predictive Analytics activities?
<--- Score

79. Is a fully trained team formed, supported, and committed to work on the Predictive Analytics improvements?
<--- Score

80. How does the Predictive Analytics manager ensure against scope creep?
<--- Score

81. Is there a completed, verified, and validated high-level 'as is' (not 'should be' or 'could be') business process map?
<--- Score

82. Does the team have regular meetings?
<--- Score

83. What is out of scope?
<--- Score

84. Why are you doing Predictive Analytics and what is the scope?

<--- Score

85. Are required metrics defined, what are they?
<--- Score

86. How will variation in the actual durations of each activity be dealt with to ensure that the expected Predictive Analytics results are met?
<--- Score

87. What system do you use for gathering Predictive Analytics information?
<--- Score

88. Is the scope of Predictive Analytics defined?
<--- Score

89. Are resources adequate for the scope?
<--- Score

90. Are improvement team members fully trained on Predictive Analytics?
<--- Score

91. Has a project plan, Gantt chart, or similar been developed/completed?
<--- Score

92. Are there any constraints known that bear on the ability to perform Predictive Analytics work? How is the team addressing them?
<--- Score

93. What is out-of-scope initially?
<--- Score

94. Have all of the relationships been defined properly?
<--- Score

95. Are business processes mapped?
<--- Score

96. Who is gathering Predictive Analytics information?
<--- Score

97. Has the Predictive Analytics work been fairly and/or equitably divided and delegated among team members who are qualified and capable to perform the work? Has everyone contributed?
<--- Score

98. What is the scope of Predictive Analytics?
<--- Score

99. What is the definition of success?
<--- Score

100. How do you model context in a computational environment?
<--- Score

101. How is the team tracking and documenting its work?
<--- Score

102. What would be the goal or target for a Predictive Analytics's improvement team?
<--- Score

103. Have all basic functions of Predictive Analytics been defined?

<--- Score

104. How did the Predictive Analytics manager receive input to the development of a Predictive Analytics improvement plan and the estimated completion dates/times of each activity?
<--- Score

105. Are roles and responsibilities formally defined?
<--- Score

106. Are audit criteria, scope, frequency and methods defined?
<--- Score

107. What is the context?
<--- Score

108. When is the estimated completion date?
<--- Score

109. Is the team equipped with available and reliable resources?
<--- Score

110. Is Predictive Analytics currently on schedule according to the plan?
<--- Score

111. What is in the scope and what is not in scope?
<--- Score

112. How often are the team meetings?
<--- Score

113. Do you all define Predictive Analytics in the same

way?
<--- Score

114. What baselines are required to be defined and managed?
<--- Score

115. Is full participation by members in regularly held team meetings guaranteed?
<--- Score

Add up total points for this section:
_____ = Total points for this section

Divided by: _____ (number of statements answered) = _____
Average score for this section

Transfer your score to the Predictive Analytics Index at the beginning of the Self-Assessment.

CRITERION #3: MEASURE:

INTENT: Gather the correct data.
Measure the current performance and
evolution of the situation.

In my belief, the answer to this
question is clearly defined:

5 Strongly Agree

4 Agree

3 Neutral

2 Disagree

1 Strongly Disagree

1. Is long term and short term variability accounted
for?
<--- Score

**2. What is the share of fixed costs in the total costs
per vehicle?**
<--- Score

3. Have the concerns of stakeholders to help identify

and define potential barriers been obtained and analyzed?

<--- Score

4. Is data collected on key measures that were identified?

<--- Score

5. Do you effectively measure and reward individual and team performance?

<--- Score

6. What are direct examples that show predictive analytics to be highly reliable?

<--- Score

7. How Do You Measure Success?

<--- Score

8. What is the right balance of time and resources between investigation, analysis, and discussion and dissemination?

<--- Score

9. How many predictive analytics functions are measured explicitly on improvement in predictive accuracy, with the CEO keeping an eye on this (retention, acquisition, risk, pricing models) ?

<--- Score

10. Is key measure data collection planned and executed, process variation displayed and communicated and performance baselined?

<--- Score

11. Does the Predictive Analytics task fit the client's

priorities?

<--- Score

12. Does Predictive Analytics systematically track and analyze outcomes for accountability and quality improvement?

<--- Score

13. Are the measurements objective?

<--- Score

14. How do you do risk analysis of rare, cascading, catastrophic events?

<--- Score

15. Who participated in the data collection for measurements?

<--- Score

16. How do you focus on what is right -not who is right?

<--- Score

17. How are measurements made?

<--- Score

18. How can you measure the performance?

<--- Score

19. Have changes been properly/adequately analyzed for effect?

<--- Score

20. Which stakeholder characteristics are analyzed?

<--- Score

21. How do you measure efficient delivery of Predictive Analytics services?
<--- Score

22. Cognitive procurement, ML, AI, Blockchain, Predictive Analytics, and RPA will have an impact on procurement. What is the technology impacting your here and now?
<--- Score

23. Does Predictive Analytics analysis isolate the fundamental causes of problems?
<--- Score

24. Are high impact defects defined and identified in the business process?
<--- Score

25. What disadvantage does this cause for the user?
<--- Score

26. What are the types and number of measures to use?
<--- Score

27. Predictive Analytics: What will happen?
<--- Score

28. Can you do Predictive Analytics without complex (expensive) analysis?
<--- Score

29. What measurements are possible, practicable and meaningful?
<--- Score

30. Are the units of measure consistent?
<--- Score

31. Which measures and indicators matter?
<--- Score

32. Is a solid data collection plan established that includes measurement systems analysis?
<--- Score

33. What charts has the team used to display the components of variation in the process?
<--- Score

34. What infrastructure do you have in place for predictive analytics?
<--- Score

35. What is measured? Why?
<--- Score

36. How do your measurements capture actionable Predictive Analytics information for use in exceeding your customers expectations and securing your customers engagement?
<--- Score

37. Is it a good idea to follow a hierarchy of descriptive and predictive analytics before applying prescriptive analytics?
<--- Score

38. How can you measure Predictive Analytics in a systematic way?
<--- Score

39. How do you aggregate measures across priorities?
<--- Score

40. Who should receive measurement reports?
<--- Score

41. Are you aware of what could cause a problem?
<--- Score

42. What is the vendor's overall approach to implementing a data analytic system?
<--- Score

43. How do you identify and analyze stakeholders and their interests?
<--- Score

44. Does Predictive Analytics analysis show the relationships among important Predictive Analytics factors?
<--- Score

45. How will you measure success?
<--- Score

46. What are your key Predictive Analytics indicators that you will measure, analyze and track?
<--- Score

47. How frequently do you track Predictive Analytics measures?
<--- Score

48. What are your customers expectations and measures?
<--- Score

49. Is Process Variation Displayed/Communicated?
<--- Score

50. Does your organization systematically track and analyze outcomes related for accountability and quality improvement?
<--- Score

51. Did you tackle the cause or the symptom?
<--- Score

52. Have all non-recommended alternatives been analyzed in sufficient detail?
<--- Score

53. What key measures identified indicate the performance of the business process?
<--- Score

54. Are there measurements based on task performance?
<--- Score

55. What causes mismanagement?
<--- Score

56. Have you found any 'ground fruit' or 'low-hanging fruit' for immediate remedies to the gap in performance?
<--- Score

57. What are your key Predictive Analytics organizational performance measures, including key short and longer-term financial measures?
<--- Score

58. What methods are feasible and acceptable to estimate the impact of reforms?
<--- Score

59. What could cause delays in the schedule?
<--- Score

60. Why do the measurements/indicators matter?
<--- Score

61. Why do you expend time and effort to implement measurement, for whom?
<--- Score

62. How will measures be used to manage and adapt?
<--- Score

63. How do you measure the efficiency of your algorithms?
<--- Score

64. Does the organization need to run in batch mode, or is there a need to run analytics in real-time and/or streaming?
<--- Score

65. In the near future, who do you expect will be using predictive analytics tools in your organization?
<--- Score

66. What could cause you to change course?
<--- Score

67. Is there a Performance Baseline?

<--- Score

68. Is it possible to estimate the impact of unanticipated complexity such as wrong or failed assumptions, feedback, etc. on proposed reforms?
<--- Score

69. How do you measure variability?
<--- Score

70. What data was collected (past, present, future/ongoing)?
<--- Score

71. What causes extra work or rework?
<--- Score

72. The approach of traditional Predictive Analytics works for detail complexity but is focused on a systematic approach rather than an understanding of the nature of systems themselves, what approach will permit your organization to deal with the kind of unpredictable emergent behaviors that dynamic complexity can introduce?
<--- Score

73. Are missed Predictive Analytics opportunities costing your organization money?
<--- Score

74. Are there any easy-to-implement alternatives to Predictive Analytics? Sometimes other solutions are available that do not require the cost implications of a full-blown project?
<--- Score

75. What types of analytics do you want?

<--- Score

76. Can you measure the return on analysis?

<--- Score

77. How is the value delivered by Predictive Analytics being measured?

<--- Score

78. How might government agencies use predictive analytics to improve operational and mission capabilities?

<--- Score

79. What causes innovation to fail or succeed in your organization?

<--- Score

80. What particular quality tools did the team find helpful in establishing measurements?

<--- Score

81. How do you control the overall costs of your work processes?

<--- Score

82. Are process variation components displayed/ communicated using suitable charts, graphs, plots?

<--- Score

83. Are there any good resources for predictive analytics that apply specifically to your organizations vertical?

<--- Score

84. What measurements are being captured?
<--- Score

85. How is performance measured?
<--- Score

86. What Is the Business Value of Predictive Analytics to Your Organization?
<--- Score

87. How is predictive analytics applied?
<--- Score

88. What are the costs of reform?
<--- Score

89. How will your organization measure success?
<--- Score

90. How will you measure your Predictive Analytics effectiveness?
<--- Score

91. How do you know that any Predictive Analytics analysis is complete and comprehensive?
<--- Score

92. How does predictive analytics help to understand the future?
<--- Score

93. How large is the gap between current performance and the customer-specified (goal) performance?
<--- Score

94. Was a data collection plan established?

<--- Score

95. What are the uncertainties surrounding estimates of impact?

<--- Score

96. Have the types of risks that may impact Predictive Analytics been identified and analyzed?

<--- Score

97. How do you stay flexible and focused to recognize larger Predictive Analytics results?

<--- Score

98. How will effects be measured?

<--- Score

99. Where is it measured?

<--- Score

100. Are you taking your company in the direction of better and revenue or cheaper and cost?

<--- Score

101. How do you measure lifecycle phases?

<--- Score

102. Do you aggressively reward and promote the people who have the biggest impact on creating excellent Predictive Analytics services/products?

<--- Score

103. What kind of data do you use for predictive analytics?

<--- Score

104. What evidence is there and what is measured?
<--- Score

105. What are the most significant challenges and opportunities in predictive analytics?
<--- Score

106. What would be a real cause for concern?
<--- Score

107. Is the solution cost-effective?
<--- Score

108. What do you measure and why?
<--- Score

109. How to cause the change?
<--- Score

110. Are losses documented, analyzed, and remedial processes developed to prevent future losses?
<--- Score

111. How will success or failure be measured?
<--- Score

112. Does Human Resources Analytics equal Predictive Analytics?
<--- Score

113. What has the team done to assure the stability and accuracy of the measurement process?
<--- Score

114. In the near future, who do you expect to be

using predictive analytics tools?
<--- Score

115. What harm might be caused?
<--- Score

116. What relevant entities could be measured?
<--- Score

117. What are the key input variables? What are
the key process variables? What are the key output
variables?
<--- Score

118. What are the agreed upon definitions of the high
impact areas, defect(s), unit(s), and opportunities that
will figure into the process capability metrics?
<--- Score

119. How is progress measured?
<--- Score

**120. Will information produced by the analytics
system be understandable to end users?**
<--- Score

121. Have you made assumptions about the shape of
the future, particularly its impact on your customers
and competitors?
<--- Score

122. What is an unallowable cost?
<--- Score

**123. How can descriptive and predictive analytics
help in pursuing prescriptive analytics?**

<--- Score

124. Do staff have the necessary skills to collect, analyze, and report data?
<--- Score

125. Are key measures identified and agreed upon?
<--- Score

126. How is predictive analytics applied in the application case?
<--- Score

127. Among the Predictive Analytics product and service cost to be estimated, which is considered hardest to estimate?
<--- Score

128. What causes investor action?
<--- Score

129. Is data collection planned and executed?
<--- Score

130. What potential environmental factors impact the Predictive Analytics effort?
<--- Score

Add up total points for this section:
_ _ _ _ _ = Total points for this section

Divided by: _ _ _ _ _ _ (number of statements answered) = _ _ _ _ _ _
Average score for this section

Transfer your score to the Predictive

Analytics Index at the beginning of the
Self-Assessment.

CRITERION #4: ANALYZE:

INTENT: Analyze causes, assumptions and hypotheses.

In my belief, the answer to this question is clearly defined:

5 Strongly Agree

4 Agree

3 Neutral

2 Disagree

1 Strongly Disagree

1. Is the required Predictive Analytics data gathered?
<--- Score

2. Were any designed experiments used to generate additional insight into the data analysis?
<--- Score

3. Which data to store?
<--- Score

4. How do you track the provenance of the derived data/information?
<--- Score

5. Is the process repeatable as you change algorithms and data structures?
<--- Score

6. What are your current levels and trends in key measures or indicators of Predictive Analytics product and process performance that are important to and directly serve your customers? How do these results compare with the performance of your competitors and other organizations with similar offerings?
<--- Score

7. What are the output interfaces to external systems?
<--- Score

8. How do you know whether a data mining solution is really needed?
<--- Score

9. How many databases do you need to pull data from?
<--- Score

10. How often will data be collected for measures?
<--- Score

11. Are Predictive Analytics changes recognized early enough to be approved through the regular process?
<--- Score

12. Do you, as a leader, bounce back quickly from

setbacks?

<--- Score

13. How fast can you adapt to changes in the data stream?

<--- Score

14. What is the limit for value as you add more data?

<--- Score

15. How often is the data in the source data warehouse and other sources of data for this application refreshed ?

<--- Score

16. What data sources to ingest?

<--- Score

17. What does the data say about the performance of the business process?

<--- Score

18. Is the gap/opportunity displayed and communicated in financial terms?

<--- Score

19. Do your employees have the opportunity to do what they do best everyday?

<--- Score

20. What data is gathered?

<--- Score

21. What were the financial benefits resulting from any 'ground fruit or low-hanging fruit' (quick fixes)?

<--- Score

22. What is data warehousing and why do you need it?
<--- Score

23. Can the data be migrated?
<--- Score

24. What data do you need to get?
<--- Score

25. Identify an operational issue in your organization. for example, could a particular task be done more quickly or more efficiently by Predictive Analytics?
<--- Score

26. What is the level of granularity of your data?
<--- Score

27. How much data is really relevant to the problem solution?
<--- Score

28. What new Security and Privacy challenge arises from the Big Data solutions you use?
<--- Score

29. What Predictive Analytics data do you gather or use now?
<--- Score

30. What are your key performance measures or indicators and in-process measures for the control and improvement of your Predictive Analytics processes?

<--- Score

31. How do you identify specific Predictive Analytics investment opportunities and emerging trends?
<--- Score

32. What were the crucial 'moments of truth' on the process map?
<--- Score

33. Have any additional benefits been identified that will result from closing all or most of the gaps?
<--- Score

34. What rules and regulations exist about combining data about individuals into a central repository?
<--- Score

35. How is the way you as the leader think and process information affecting your organizational culture?
<--- Score

36. How was the detailed process map generated, verified, and validated?
<--- Score

37. Do several people in different organizational units assist with the Predictive Analytics process?
<--- Score

38. Did any additional data need to be collected?
<--- Score

39. How do your work systems and key work processes relate to and capitalize on your core

competencies?

<--- Score

40. Where is the data coming from to measure compliance?

<--- Score

41. Think about the functions involved in your Predictive Analytics project, what processes flow from these functions?

<--- Score

42. Think about some of the processes you undertake within your organization, which do you own?

<--- Score

43. Can you use data without the permission of individual owners, such as copying publicly available data?

<--- Score

44. What successful thing are you doing today that may be blinding you to new growth opportunities?

<--- Score

45. Why is it that you are talking about data mining now?

<--- Score

46. What will drive Predictive Analytics change?

<--- Score

47. How will the DSS fit into the decision-making process?

<--- Score

48. Did any value-added analysis or 'lean thinking' take place to identify some of the gaps shown on the 'as is' process map?

<--- Score

49. How do you use Predictive Analytics data and information to support organizational decision making and innovation?

<--- Score

50. What conclusions were drawn from the team's data collection and analysis? How did the team reach these conclusions?

<--- Score

51. How do you implement and manage your work processes to ensure that they meet design requirements?

<--- Score

52. What tools were used to narrow the list of possible causes?

<--- Score

53. What tools were used to generate the list of possible causes?

<--- Score

54. What is your organizations process which leads to recognition of value generation?

<--- Score

55. How much data correction can you do at the edges?

<--- Score

56. What methods do you use to gather Predictive Analytics data?

<--- Score

57. Record-keeping requirements flow from the records needed as inputs, outputs, controls and for transformation of a Predictive Analytics process. Are the records needed as inputs to the Predictive Analytics process available?

<--- Score

58. What other organizational variables, such as reward systems or communication systems, affect the performance of this Predictive Analytics process?

<--- Score

59. Who has access to data?

<--- Score

60. Do your contracts/agreements contain data security obligations?

<--- Score

61. How do you measure the operational performance of your key work systems and processes, including productivity, cycle time, and other appropriate measures of process effectiveness, efficiency, and innovation?

<--- Score

62. A compounding model resolution with available relevant data can often provide insight towards a solution methodology; which Predictive Analytics models, tools and techniques are necessary?

<--- Score

63. What parts of the decision-making process will be supported by the system?

<--- Score

64. Is Data and process analysis, root cause analysis and quantifying the gap/opportunity in place?

<--- Score

65. What are the revised rough estimates of the financial savings/opportunity for Predictive Analytics improvements?

<--- Score

66. Was a detailed process map created to amplify critical steps of the 'as is' business process?

<--- Score

67. What are the best opportunities for value improvement?

<--- Score

68. How can the benefits of Big Data collection and applications be measured?

<--- Score

69. Is the suppliers process defined and controlled?

<--- Score

70. How do mission and objectives affect the Predictive Analytics processes of your organization?

<--- Score

71. Were there any improvement opportunities identified from the process analysis?

<--- Score

72. What are your best practices for minimizing Predictive Analytics project risk, while demonstrating incremental value and quick wins throughout the Predictive Analytics project lifecycle?

<--- Score

73. Can you add value to the current Predictive Analytics decision-making process (largely qualitative) by incorporating uncertainty modeling (more quantitative)?

<--- Score

74. What are the drivers for actual user adoption of the technology?

<--- Score

75. What if the needle happens to be a complex data structure?

<--- Score

76. What attributes define Big Data solutions?

<--- Score

77. Do you need to process X amount of data in X amount of time?

<--- Score

78. How fast can you determine changes in the incoming data?

<--- Score

79. What is the cost of poor quality as supported by the team's analysis?

<--- Score

80. What is next for big data applications?

<--- Score

81. How do you promote understanding that opportunity for improvement is not criticism of the status quo, or the people who created the status quo?
<--- Score

82. Was a cause-and-effect diagram used to explore the different types of causes (or sources of variation)?
<--- Score

83. Is the performance gap determined?
<--- Score

84. Have the problem and goal statements been updated to reflect the additional knowledge gained from the analyze phase?
<--- Score

85. What process should you select for improvement?
<--- Score

86. What are your current levels and trends in key Predictive Analytics measures or indicators of product and process performance that are important to and directly serve your customers?
<--- Score

87. Is the Predictive Analytics process severely broken such that a re-design is necessary?
<--- Score

88. Can good algorithms, models, heuristics overcome data quality problems?
<--- Score

89. Are gaps between current performance and the goal performance identified?
<--- Score

90. What other jobs or tasks affect the performance of the steps in the Predictive Analytics process?
<--- Score

91. What are your Predictive Analytics processes?
<--- Score

92. How is Predictive Analytics data gathered?
<--- Score

93. An organizationally feasible system request is one that considers the mission, goals and objectives of the organization. Key questions are: is the Predictive Analytics solution request practical and will it solve a problem or take advantage of an opportunity to achieve company goals?
<--- Score

94. How do you identify relevant fragments of data easily from a multitude of data sources?
<--- Score

95. What controls do you have in place to protect data?
<--- Score

96. Requirements: What does the business want from the data warehouse?
<--- Score

97. What is the contribution of subsets of the data to the problem solution?

<--- Score

98. How is Big Data different from traditional data environments and related applications?
<--- Score

99. Were Pareto charts (or similar) used to portray the 'heavy hitters' (or key sources of variation)?
<--- Score

100. Are you required to inform individuals when you use data?
<--- Score

101. How much value is created for each unit of data?
<--- Score

102. What preprocessing do you need to do?
<--- Score

103. Do your leaders quickly bounce back from setbacks?
<--- Score

104. What is the current state of the data?
<--- Score

105. How will your systems and methods evolve to remove Big Data solution weaknesses?
<--- Score

106. Where is Predictive Analytics data gathered?
<--- Score

107. What did the team gain from developing a sub-

process map?
<--- Score

108. What are the new developments that are included in Big Data solutions?
<--- Score

109. Do you have relations with organizations in terms of abilities to leverage big data in the supply chain?
<--- Score

110. What are the new applications that are enabled by Big Data solutions?
<--- Score

111. How long should data be stored?
<--- Score

112. What quality tools were used to get through the analyze phase?
<--- Score

113. How can the best Big Data solution be chosen based on use case requirements?
<--- Score

114. How does the organization define, manage, and improve its Predictive Analytics processes?
<--- Score

Add up total points for this section:
_ _ _ _ _ = Total points for this section

Divided by: _ _ _ _ _ _ (number of statements answered) = _ _ _ _ _ _

Average score for this section

Transfer your score to the Predictive
Analytics Index at the beginning of the
Self-Assessment.

CRITERION #5: IMPROVE:

INTENT: Develop a practical solution. Innovate, establish and test the solution and to measure the results.

In my belief, the answer to this question is clearly defined:

5 Strongly Agree

4 Agree

3 Neutral

2 Disagree

1 Strongly Disagree

1. How significant is the improvement in the eyes of the end user?
<--- Score

2. What results can you expect?
<--- Score

3. Which of the recognised risks out of all risks can be most likely transferred?

<--- Score

4. How will you know when its improved?
<--- Score

5. What is Predictive Analytics's impact on utilizing the best solution(s)?
<--- Score

6. How do you measure risk?
<--- Score

7. What attendant changes will need to be made to ensure that the solution is successful?
<--- Score

8. Was a pilot designed for the proposed solution(s)?
<--- Score

9. What are the implications of the one critical Predictive Analytics decision 10 minutes, 10 months, and 10 years from now?
<--- Score

10. Are possible solutions generated and tested?
<--- Score

11. Do those selected for the Predictive Analytics team have a good general understanding of what Predictive Analytics is all about?
<--- Score

12. How did the team generate the list of possible solutions?
<--- Score

13. Are you assessing Predictive Analytics and risk?
<--- Score

14. Is the optimal solution selected based on testing and analysis?
<--- Score

15. Risk events: what are the things that could go wrong?
<--- Score

16. What resources are required for the improvement efforts?
<--- Score

17. What communications are necessary to support the implementation of the solution?
<--- Score

18. What are your current levels and trends in key measures or indicators of workforce and leader development?
<--- Score

19. What do you want to improve?
<--- Score

20. Is the scope clearly documented?
<--- Score

21. What does the 'should be' process map/design look like?
<--- Score

22. How will the team or the process owner(s) monitor the implementation plan to see that it is working as

intended?
<--- Score

23. What improvements have been achieved?
<--- Score

24. What needs improvement? Why?
<--- Score

25. How do you define the solutions' scope?
<--- Score

26. Are risk triggers captured?
<--- Score

27. How do you improve your likelihood of success ?
<--- Score

28. Does the goal represent a desired result that can be measured?
<--- Score

29. What actually has to improve and by how much?
<--- Score

30. Explorations of the frontiers of Predictive Analytics will help you build influence, improve Predictive Analytics, optimize decision making, and sustain change, what is your approach?
<--- Score

31. How can skill-level changes improve Predictive Analytics?
<--- Score

32. Are new and improved process ('should be') maps

developed?
<--- Score

33. What can you do to improve?
<--- Score

34. What error proofing will be done to address some of the discrepancies observed in the 'as is' process?
<--- Score

35. Is the measure of success for Predictive Analytics understandable to a variety of people?
<--- Score

36. Is there a high likelihood that any recommendations will achieve their intended results?
<--- Score

37. How do you improve productivity?
<--- Score

38. Is the implementation plan designed?
<--- Score

39. How do you go about comparing Predictive Analytics approaches/solutions?
<--- Score

40. If you could go back in time five years, what decision would you make differently? What is your best guess as to what decision you're making today you might regret five years from now?
<--- Score

41. Can you identify any significant risks or exposures to Predictive Analytics third- parties (vendors, service

providers, alliance partners etc) that concern you?
<--- Score

42. What to do with the results or outcomes of measurements?
<--- Score

43. Is the solution technically practical?
<--- Score

44. What tools were used to evaluate the potential solutions?
<--- Score

45. Do you get the same results from the different sources?
<--- Score

46. Who controls the risk?
<--- Score

47. How will you measure the results?
<--- Score

48. Is a solution implementation plan established, including schedule/work breakdown structure, resources, risk management plan, cost/budget, and control plan?
<--- Score

49. What decisions need support?
<--- Score

50. For decision problems, how do you develop a decision statement?
<--- Score

51. What practices helps your organization to develop its capacity to recognize patterns?
<--- Score

52. What is the magnitude of the improvements?
<--- Score

53. Are the best solutions selected?
<--- Score

54. What lessons, if any, from a pilot were incorporated into the design of the full-scale solution?
<--- Score

55. Describe the design of the pilot and what tests were conducted, if any?
<--- Score

56. What is the implementation plan?
<--- Score

57. How will you know that you have improved?
<--- Score

58. Who will be responsible for making the decisions to include or exclude requested changes once Predictive Analytics is underway?
<--- Score

59. How do you improve Predictive Analytics service perception, and satisfaction?
<--- Score

60. For estimation problems, how do you develop an estimation statement?

<--- Score

61. How do the Predictive Analytics results compare with the performance of your competitors and other organizations with similar offerings?
<--- Score

62. What factors and attributes will determine your organizations success in this development?
<--- Score

63. Risk Identification: What are the possible risk events your organization faces in relation to Predictive Analytics?
<--- Score

64. What is the team's contingency plan for potential problems occurring in implementation?
<--- Score

65. Are improved process ('should be') maps modified based on pilot data and analysis?
<--- Score

66. Who will be responsible for documenting the Predictive Analytics requirements in detail?
<--- Score

67. Is there a cost/benefit analysis of optimal solution(s)?
<--- Score

68. What is the Predictive Analytics's sustainability risk?
<--- Score

69. How do you link measurement and risk?
<--- Score

70. What went well, what should change, what can improve?
<--- Score

71. How do you measure progress and evaluate training effectiveness?
<--- Score

72. Risk factors: what are the characteristics of Predictive Analytics that make it risky?
<--- Score

73. Is there a small-scale pilot for proposed improvement(s)? What conclusions were drawn from the outcomes of a pilot?
<--- Score

74. Who controls key decisions that will be made?
<--- Score

75. Is pilot data collected and analyzed?
<--- Score

76. How do you measure improved Predictive Analytics service perception, and satisfaction?
<--- Score

77. How does the team improve its work?
<--- Score

78. To what extent does management recognize Predictive Analytics as a tool to increase the results?
<--- Score

79. How do the new developments address the issues of needed capacity and capability?
<--- Score

80. What tools were most useful during the improve phase?
<--- Score

81. What is the risk?
<--- Score

82. Can the solution be designed and implemented within an acceptable time period?
<--- Score

83. How do you manage and improve your Predictive Analytics work systems to deliver customer value and achieve organizational success and sustainability?
<--- Score

84. How can you improve Predictive Analytics?
<--- Score

85. Who will be using the results of the measurement activities?
<--- Score

86. How do you keep improving Predictive Analytics?
<--- Score

87. Is supporting Predictive Analytics documentation required?
<--- Score

88. Will the controls trigger any other risks?

<--- Score

89. How will the organization know that the solution worked?
<--- Score

90. Who are the people involved in developing and implementing Predictive Analytics?
<--- Score

91. In the past few months, what is the smallest change you have made that has had the biggest positive result? What was it about that small change that produced the large return?
<--- Score

92. What tools were used to tap into the creativity and encourage 'outside the box' thinking?
<--- Score

93. How can you improve performance?
<--- Score

94. Were any criteria developed to assist the team in testing and evaluating potential solutions?
<--- Score

95. Why improve in the first place?
<--- Score

96. Are there any constraints (technical, political, cultural, or otherwise) that would inhibit certain solutions?
<--- Score

97. What were the underlying assumptions on the

cost-benefit analysis?

<--- Score

98. How will you know that a change is an improvement?

<--- Score

99. Is a contingency plan established?

<--- Score

100. How does the solution remove the key sources of issues discovered in the analyze phase?

<--- Score

Add up total points for this section:

_____ = Total points for this section

Divided by: _____ (number of statements answered) = _____ Average score for this section

Transfer your score to the Predictive Analytics Index at the beginning of the Self-Assessment.

CRITERION #6: CONTROL:

In my belief, the answer to this question is clearly defined:

5 Strongly Agree

4 Agree

3 Neutral

2 Disagree

1 Strongly Disagree

1. Can support from partners be adjusted?
<--- Score

2. Is there a recommended audit plan for routine surveillance inspections of Predictive Analytics's gains?
<--- Score

3. Are new process steps, standards, and

documentation ingrained into normal operations?
<--- Score

4. How will new or emerging customer needs/
requirements be checked/communicated to orient
the process toward meeting the new specifications
and continually reducing variation?
<--- Score

5. Does the response plan contain a definite closed
loop continual improvement scheme (e.g., plan-do-
check-act)?
<--- Score

6. What key inputs and outputs are being measured
on an ongoing basis?
<--- Score

7. How will you measure your QA plan's effectiveness?
<--- Score

8. What is the recommended frequency of auditing?
<--- Score

9. Is there a control plan in place for sustaining
improvements (short and long-term)?
<--- Score

10. What adjustments to the strategies are needed?
<--- Score

11. How do you encourage people to take control and
responsibility?
<--- Score

12. Is there a transfer of ownership and knowledge

to process owner and process team tasked with the responsibilities.
<--- Score

13. How will the process owner and team be able to hold the gains?
<--- Score

14. Does job training on the documented procedures need to be part of the process team's education and training?
<--- Score

15. What are the critical parameters to watch?
<--- Score

16. How do you select, collect, align, and integrate Predictive Analytics data and information for tracking daily operations and overall organizational performance, including progress relative to strategic objectives and action plans?
<--- Score

17. What should you measure to verify efficiency gains?
<--- Score

18. Are there documented procedures?
<--- Score

19. How will the day-to-day responsibilities for monitoring and continual improvement be transferred from the improvement team to the process owner?
<--- Score

20. What quality tools were useful in the control phase?
<--- Score

21. How can you best use all of your knowledge repositories to enhance learning and sharing?
<--- Score

22. What do your reports reflect?
<--- Score

23. Act/Adjust: What Do you Need to Do Differently?
<--- Score

24. How do senior leaders actions reflect a commitment to the organizations Predictive Analytics values?
<--- Score

25. Who controls critical resources?
<--- Score

26. Is the range of stakeholder goals and values identified and reflected?
<--- Score

27. How do you monitor changes in the supply chain environment?
<--- Score

28. What is your theory of human motivation, and how does your compensation plan fit with that view?
<--- Score

29. What can you control?
<--- Score

30. What is the control/monitoring plan?
<--- Score

31. Who is the Predictive Analytics process owner?
<--- Score

32. Is there a documented and implemented monitoring plan?
<--- Score

33. Do you monitor the Predictive Analytics decisions made and fine tune them as they evolve?
<--- Score

34. Which processing. monitoring, and management tools are necessary?
<--- Score

35. What are you attempting to measure/monitor?
<--- Score

36. Is a response plan established and deployed?
<--- Score

37. What are the key elements of your Predictive Analytics performance improvement system, including your evaluation, organizational learning, and innovation processes?
<--- Score

38. How do you plan on providing proper recognition and disclosure of supporting companies?
<--- Score

39. Are suggested corrective/restorative actions

indicated on the response plan for known causes to problems that might surface?

<--- Score

40. Are you measuring, monitoring and predicting Predictive Analytics activities to optimize operations and profitability, and enhancing outcomes?

<--- Score

41. Are documented procedures clear and easy to follow for the operators?

<--- Score

42. Does Predictive Analytics appropriately measure and monitor risk?

<--- Score

43. You may have created your quality measures at a time when you lacked resources, technology wasn't up to the required standard, or low service levels were the industry norm. Have those circumstances changed?

<--- Score

44. Is there documentation that will support the successful operation of the improvement?

<--- Score

45. In the case of a Predictive Analytics project, the criteria for the audit derive from implementation objectives. an audit of a Predictive Analytics project involves assessing whether the recommendations outlined for implementation have been met. Can you track that any Predictive Analytics project is implemented as planned, and is it working?

<--- Score

46. Are the planned controls working?
<--- Score

47. What is the best design framework for Predictive Analytics organization now that, in a post industrial-age if the top-down, command and control model is no longer relevant?
<--- Score

48. Who has control over resources?
<--- Score

49. How is change control managed?
<--- Score

50. Where do ideas that reach policy makers and planners as proposals for Predictive Analytics strengthening and reform actually originate?
<--- Score

51. What other areas of the organization might benefit from the Predictive Analytics team's improvements, knowledge, and learning?
<--- Score

52. Can you adapt and adjust to changing Predictive Analytics situations?
<--- Score

53. What do you measure to verify effectiveness gains?
<--- Score

54. Is knowledge gained on process shared and institutionalized?

<--- Score

55. Will any special training be provided for results interpretation?
<--- Score

56. What are the known security controls?
<--- Score

57. What kinds of predictive analytics and machine learning would you look for?
<--- Score

58. Who will be in control?
<--- Score

59. Are there any best practices or standards for the use of Big Data solutions?
<--- Score

60. Does the Predictive Analytics performance meet the customer's requirements?
<--- Score

61. Does a troubleshooting guide exist or is it needed?
<--- Score

62. For social media in a business context what differences are there between social media monitoring text analytics and predictive analytics tools?
<--- Score

63. How will report readings be checked to effectively monitor performance?
<--- Score

64. Do the Predictive Analytics decisions you make today help people and the planet tomorrow?
<--- Score

65. Implementation Planning: is a pilot needed to test the changes before a full roll out occurs?
<--- Score

66. Are the planned controls in place?
<--- Score

67. Who sets the Predictive Analytics standards?
<--- Score

68. What do you stand for--and what are you against?
<--- Score

69. What other systems, operations, processes, and infrastructures (hiring practices, staffing, training, incentives/rewards, metrics/dashboards/scorecards, etc.) need updates, additions, changes, or deletions in order to facilitate knowledge transfer and improvements?
<--- Score

70. Will the team be available to assist members in planning investigations?
<--- Score

71. Is reporting being used or needed?
<--- Score

72. Is new knowledge gained imbedded in the response plan?
<--- Score

73. Are pertinent alerts monitored, analyzed and distributed to appropriate personnel?
<--- Score

74. How do you establish and deploy modified action plans if circumstances require a shift in plans and rapid execution of new plans?
<--- Score

75. How will input, process, and output variables be checked to detect for sub-optimal conditions?
<--- Score

76. Is a response plan in place for when the input, process, or output measures indicate an 'out-of-control' condition?
<--- Score

77. How do controls support value?
<--- Score

78. What should the next improvement project be that is related to Predictive Analytics?
<--- Score

79. Is there a standardized process?
<--- Score

80. Are operating procedures consistent?
<--- Score

81. How do your controls stack up?
<--- Score

82. How might the organization capture best practices

and lessons learned so as to leverage improvements across the business?
<--- Score

83. Has the improved process and its steps been standardized?
<--- Score

84. Have new or revised work instructions resulted?
<--- Score

85. Are controls in place and consistently applied?
<--- Score

86. Will your goals reflect your program budget?
<--- Score

87. Is there a Predictive Analytics Communication plan covering who needs to get what information when?
<--- Score

88. How likely is the current Predictive Analytics plan to come in on schedule or on budget?
<--- Score

89. Against what alternative is success being measured?
<--- Score

90. How will the process owner verify improvement in present and future sigma levels, process capabilities?
<--- Score

91. Do you monitor the effectiveness of your Predictive Analytics activities?
<--- Score

Add up total points for this section:
_____ = Total points for this section

Divided by: _____ (number of
statements answered) = _____
Average score for this section

Transfer your score to the Predictive
Analytics Index at the beginning of the
Self-Assessment.

CRITERION #7: SUSTAIN:

INTENT: Retain the benefits.

In my belief, the answer to this
question is clearly defined:

5 Strongly Agree

4 Agree

3 Neutral

2 Disagree

1 Strongly Disagree

1. What are you trying to model?
<--- Score

2. What unique value proposition (UVP) do you offer?
<--- Score

3. What are specific Predictive Analytics rules to
follow?
<--- Score

4. What is tacit permission and approval to you?

<--- Score

5. Who is on the team?
<--- Score

6. What are you trying to prove to yourself, and how might it be hijacking your life and business success?
<--- Score

7. Who are your customers?
<--- Score

8. What are the usability implications of Predictive Analytics actions?
<--- Score

9. What is the most important factor in vendor selection?
<--- Score

10. What must you excel at?
<--- Score

11. Why do and why don't your customers like your organization?
<--- Score

12. Marketing budgets are tighter, consumers are more skeptical, and social media has changed forever the way we talk about Predictive Analytics. How do you gain traction?
<--- Score

13. How do you engage the workforce, in addition to satisfying them?
<--- Score

14. What business benefits will Predictive Analytics goals deliver if achieved?

<--- Score

15. Are you / should you be revolutionary or evolutionary?

<--- Score

16. What do we do when new problems arise?

<--- Score

17. Are the assumptions believable and achievable?

<--- Score

18. How long will it take to change?

<--- Score

19. How will you ensure you get what you expected?

<--- Score

20. If you do not follow, then how to lead?

<--- Score

21. Are there any disadvantages to implementing Predictive Analytics? There might be some that are less obvious?

<--- Score

22. Is maximizing Predictive Analytics protection the same as minimizing Predictive Analytics loss?

<--- Score

23. What is it like to work for you?

<--- Score

24. How do you know if you are successful?
<--- Score

25. What are internal and external Predictive Analytics relations?
<--- Score

26. Which Predictive Analytics goals are the most important?
<--- Score

27. Do you have an implicit bias for capital investments over people investments?
<--- Score

28. In a project to restructure Predictive Analytics outcomes, which stakeholders would you involve?
<--- Score

29. Who have you, as a company, historically been when you've been at your best?
<--- Score

30. Have benefits been optimized with all key stakeholders?
<--- Score

31. Who, on the executive team or the board, has spoken to a customer recently?
<--- Score

32. Are the criteria for selecting recommendations stated?
<--- Score

33. Are you maintaining a past–present–future

perspective throughout the Predictive Analytics discussion?

<--- Score

34. Does the user interface function as intended?

<--- Score

35. How Many Variables Do You Use in Your Models?

<--- Score

36. What outcomes does your organization want to achieve by implementing the model?

<--- Score

37. Which models, tools and techniques are necessary?

<--- Score

38. If your customer were your grandmother, would you tell her to buy what you're selling?

<--- Score

39. What are the top 3 things at the forefront of your Predictive Analytics agendas for the next 3 years?

<--- Score

40. Will there be any necessary staff changes (redundancies or new hires)?

<--- Score

41. So could computers be successfully programmed to think, feel, or become truly intelligent?

<--- Score

42. What are the long-term Predictive Analytics goals?
<--- Score

43. What kind of model do you use?
<--- Score

44. How do you lead with Predictive Analytics in mind?
<--- Score

45. How do you set Predictive Analytics stretch targets and how do you get people to not only participate in setting these stretch targets but also that they strive to achieve these?
<--- Score

46. What are the short and long-term Predictive Analytics goals?
<--- Score

47. Which individuals, teams or departments will be involved in Predictive Analytics?
<--- Score

48. How do customers see your organization?
<--- Score

49. What is the recommended frequency of auditing?
<--- Score

50. In retrospect, of the projects that you pulled the plug on, what percent do you wish had been allowed to keep going, and what percent do you wish had ended earlier?
<--- Score

51. Would you rather sell to knowledgeable and informed customers or to uninformed customers?
<--- Score

52. Who do you want your customers to become?
<--- Score

53. What have been your experiences in defining long range Predictive Analytics goals?
<--- Score

54. Do you think you know, or do you know you know ?
<--- Score

55. What information is critical to your organization that your executives are ignoring?
<--- Score

56. How do you stay inspired?
<--- Score

57. Do you see more potential in people than they do in themselves?
<--- Score

58. What are current Predictive Analytics paradigms?
<--- Score

59. Can you break it down?
<--- Score

60. Do you have enough freaky customers in your portfolio pushing you to the limit day in and day out?
<--- Score

61. Will the load be even across all months or is it anticipated to peak in some months ?
<--- Score

62. What is the funding source for this project?
<--- Score

63. What are the essentials of internal Predictive Analytics management?
<--- Score

64. What one word do you want to own in the minds of your customers, employees, and partners?
<--- Score

65. Do you have past Predictive Analytics successes?
<--- Score

66. What is the craziest thing you can do?
<--- Score

67. How important is Predictive Analytics to the user organizations mission?
<--- Score

68. What will be the consequences to the stakeholder (financial, reputation etc) if Predictive Analytics does not go ahead or fails to deliver the objectives?
<--- Score

69. What may be the consequences for the performance of an organization if all stakeholders are not consulted regarding Predictive Analytics?
<--- Score

70. How do you maintain Predictive Analytics's

Integrity?
<--- Score

71. What role does communication play in the success or failure of a Predictive Analytics project?
<--- Score

72. Do you say no to customers for no reason?
<--- Score

73. What is the estimated value of the project?
<--- Score

74. Are you paying enough attention to the partners your company depends on to succeed?
<--- Score

75. When information truly is ubiquitous, when reach and connectivity are completely global, when computing resources are infinite, and when a whole new set of impossibilities are not only possible, but happening, what will that do to your business?
<--- Score

76. How will you motivate the stakeholders with the least vested interest?
<--- Score

77. Is it economical; do you have the time and money?
<--- Score

78. Do you have the heart of a scientist or a businessperson?
<--- Score

79. Who will determine interim and final deadlines?

<--- Score

80. Have new benefits been realized?
<--- Score

81. Will it be accepted by users?
<--- Score

82. At what moment would you think; Will I get fired?
<--- Score

83. Who are the key stakeholders?
<--- Score

84. What trouble can you get into?
<--- Score

85. Is there a work around that you can use?
<--- Score

86. What happens when systems approach the level of human intelligence?
<--- Score

87. How likely is it that a customer would recommend your company to a friend or colleague?
<--- Score

88. Do you think Predictive Analytics accomplishes the goals you expect it to accomplish?
<--- Score

89. Whom among your colleagues do you trust, and for what?
<--- Score

90. What is knowledge management?
<--- Score

91. Think of your Predictive Analytics project, what are the main functions?
<--- Score

92. Operational - will it work?
<--- Score

93. Who is responsible for errors?
<--- Score

94. What is a feasible sequencing of reform initiatives over time?
<--- Score

95. Instead of going to current contacts for new ideas, what if you reconnected with dormant contacts-- the people you used to know? If you were going reactivate a dormant tie, who would it be?
<--- Score

96. What are the success criteria that will indicate that Predictive Analytics objectives have been met and the benefits delivered?
<--- Score

97. Are you satisfied with your current role? If not, what is missing from it?
<--- Score

98. What relationships among Predictive Analytics trends do you perceive?
<--- Score

99. What are the potential basics of Predictive Analytics fraud?
<--- Score

100. Why should people listen to you?
<--- Score

101. Have you seen a pattern before?
<--- Score

102. Do Predictive Analytics rules make a reasonable demand on a users capabilities?
<--- Score

103. Are you changing as fast as the world around you?
<--- Score

104. Who is responsible for Predictive Analytics?
<--- Score

105. What is your question? Why?
<--- Score

106. What would have to be true for the option on the table to be the best possible choice?
<--- Score

107. What current systems have to be understood and/or changed?
<--- Score

108. What are your most important goals for the strategic Predictive Analytics objectives?
<--- Score

109. What is effective Predictive Analytics?
<--- Score

110. Who is responsible for ensuring appropriate resources (time, people and money) are allocated to Predictive Analytics?
<--- Score

111. How do you ensure that implementations of Predictive Analytics products are done in a way that ensures safety?
<--- Score

112. What level of customization within the program is possible?
<--- Score

113. What happens at your organization when people fail?
<--- Score

114. Is your basic point _____ or _____?
<--- Score

115. What are the rules and assumptions your industry operates under? What if the opposite were true?
<--- Score

116. Can you maintain your growth without detracting from the factors that have contributed to your success?
<--- Score

117. If you had to leave your organization for a year and the only communication you could have with employees/colleagues was a single paragraph, what

would you write?

<--- Score

118. What trophy do you want on your mantle?

<--- Score

119. How do you deal with Predictive Analytics changes?

<--- Score

120. Where can you break convention?

<--- Score

121. What was the last experiment you ran?

<--- Score

122. What Predictive Analytics skills are most important?

<--- Score

123. Are all key stakeholders present at all Structured Walkthroughs?

<--- Score

124. What are your personal philosophies regarding Predictive Analytics and how do they influence your work?

<--- Score

125. What new services of functionality will be implemented next with Predictive Analytics ?

<--- Score

126. Who do you think the world wants your organization to be?

<--- Score

127. What stupid rule would you most like to kill?
<--- Score

128. If no one would ever find out about your accomplishments, how would you lead differently?
<--- Score

129. What is your BATNA (best alternative to a negotiated agreement)?
<--- Score

130. What is something you believe that nearly no one agrees with you on?
<--- Score

131. What are strategies for increasing support and reducing opposition?
<--- Score

132. What are the barriers to increased Predictive Analytics production?
<--- Score

133. Is a Predictive Analytics team work effort in place?
<--- Score

134. What Is Business Intelligence?
<--- Score

135. How do you assess the Predictive Analytics pitfalls that are inherent in implementing it?
<--- Score

136. Why not do Predictive Analytics?

<--- Score

137. What have you done to protect your business from competitive encroachment?
<--- Score

138. Is Predictive Analytics dependent on the successful delivery of a current project?
<--- Score

139. What counts that you are not counting?
<--- Score

140. Ask yourself: how would you do this work if you only had one staff member to do it?
<--- Score

141. What kind of end users are anticipated to use this system ?
<--- Score

142. What Predictive Analytics modifications can you make work for you?
<--- Score

143. What are the business goals Predictive Analytics is aiming to achieve?
<--- Score

144. How do you transition from the baseline to the target?
<--- Score

145. Are assumptions made in Predictive Analytics stated explicitly?
<--- Score

146. Is the Predictive Analytics organization completing tasks effectively and efficiently?
<--- Score

147. Is the impact that Predictive Analytics has shown?
<--- Score

148. What is your formula for success in Predictive Analytics ?
<--- Score

149. What does your signature ensure?
<--- Score

150. Who will provide the final approval of Predictive Analytics deliverables?
<--- Score

151. What kind of crime could a potential new hire have committed that would not only not disqualify him/her from being hired by your organization, but would actually indicate that he/she might be a particularly good fit?
<--- Score

152. How do you keep the momentum going?
<--- Score

153. What management system can you use to leverage the Predictive Analytics experience, ideas, and concerns of the people closest to the work to be done?
<--- Score

154. What threat is Predictive Analytics addressing?
<--- Score

155. How does Predictive Analytics integrate with other business initiatives?
<--- Score

156. Has implementation been effective in reaching specified objectives so far?
<--- Score

157. What happens when a new employee joins the organization?
<--- Score

158. Whose voice (department, ethnic group, women, older workers, etc) might you have missed hearing from in your company, and how might you amplify this voice to create positive momentum for your business?
<--- Score

159. How do you make it meaningful in connecting Predictive Analytics with what users do day-to-day?
<--- Score

160. How do you keep records, of what?
<--- Score

161. Can the schedule be done in the given time?
<--- Score

162. How can you become more high-tech but still be high touch?
<--- Score

163. How close to the edge can you push the filtering and compression algorithms?
<--- Score

164. What is the range of capabilities?
<--- Score

165. How do you provide a safe environment -physically and emotionally?
<--- Score

166. What projects are going on in the organization today, and what resources are those projects using from the resource pools?
<--- Score

167. How do you listen to customers to obtain actionable information?
<--- Score

168. Who will manage the integration of tools?
<--- Score

169. How do you track customer value, profitability or financial return, organizational success, and sustainability?
<--- Score

170. Who else should you help?
<--- Score

171. How much does Predictive Analytics help?
<--- Score

172. What are the key enablers to make this Predictive Analytics move?

<--- Score

173. How do you create buy-in?
<--- Score

174. If you were responsible for initiating and implementing major changes in your organization, what steps might you take to ensure acceptance of those changes?
<--- Score

175. What are the disruptive innovations in the middle-term that provide near-term domain leadership?
<--- Score

176. Why will customers want to buy your organizations products/services?
<--- Score

177. Are new benefits received and understood?
<--- Score

178. Who are four people whose careers you have enhanced?
<--- Score

179. What happens if you do not have enough funding?
<--- Score

180. What goals did you miss?
<--- Score

181. Do you have the right capabilities and capacities?
<--- Score

182. If there were zero limitations, what would you do differently?

<--- Score

183. Can you do all this work?

<--- Score

184. How can you negotiate Predictive Analytics successfully with a stubborn boss, an irate client, or a deceitful coworker?

<--- Score

185. Why is Predictive Analytics important for you now?

<--- Score

186. What should you stop doing?

<--- Score

187. Political -is anyone trying to undermine this project?

<--- Score

188. What did you miss in the interview for the worst hire you ever made?

<--- Score

189. If your company went out of business tomorrow, would anyone who doesn't get a paycheck here care?

<--- Score

190. Who do we want your customers to become?

<--- Score

191. How can you incorporate support to ensure

safe and effective use of Predictive Analytics into the
services that you provide?

<--- Score

192. Is there any reason to believe the opposite of my
current belief?

<--- Score

193. How do you determine the key elements that
affect Predictive Analytics workforce satisfaction, how
are these elements determined for different workforce
groups and segments?

<--- Score

194. What is an unauthorized commitment?

<--- Score

**195. What kind of projects are expected in the
future?**

<--- Score

196. In the past year, what have you done (or could
you have done) to increase the accurate perception of
your company/brand as ethical and honest?

<--- Score

197. Why should you adopt a Predictive Analytics
framework?

<--- Score

198. What is the kind of project structure that would
be appropriate for your Predictive Analytics project,
should it be formal and complex, or can it be less
formal and relatively simple?

<--- Score

199. What do you expect?
<--- Score

200. What are the most efficient ways to create the models?
<--- Score

201. Are you relevant? Will you be relevant five years from now? Ten?
<--- Score

202. Are your responses positive or negative?
<--- Score

203. How are you doing compared to your industry?
<--- Score

204. Is it useful?
<--- Score

205. What are the challenges?
<--- Score

206. To whom do you add value?
<--- Score

207. Why is knowledge management important?
<--- Score

208. Do you have the right people on the bus?
<--- Score

209. What are you challenging?
<--- Score

210. Why is it important to have senior management

support for a Predictive Analytics project?

<--- Score

211. If you got fired and a new hire took your place, what would she do different?

<--- Score

212. How can you become the company that would put you out of business?

<--- Score

213. How do you accomplish your long range Predictive Analytics goals?

<--- Score

214. What is the purpose of Predictive Analytics in relation to the mission?

<--- Score

215. Who is the main stakeholder, with ultimate responsibility for driving Predictive Analytics forward?

<--- Score

216. How do you decide how much to remunerate an employee?

<--- Score

217. Who will be responsible for deciding whether Predictive Analytics goes ahead or not after the initial investigations?

<--- Score

218. How will you insure seamless interoperability of Predictive Analytics moving forward?

<--- Score

219. How do you proactively clarify deliverables and Predictive Analytics quality expectations?

<--- Score

220. How will you know that the Predictive Analytics project has been successful?

<--- Score

221. How much contingency will be available in the budget?

<--- Score

222. How is implementation research currently incorporated into each of your goals?

<--- Score

223. Are you making progress, and are you making progress as Predictive Analytics leaders?

<--- Score

224. What is the source of the strategies for Predictive Analytics strengthening and reform?

<--- Score

225. How do you foster the skills, knowledge, talents, attributes, and characteristics you want to have?

<--- Score

226. If you weren't already in this business, would you enter it today? And if not, what are you going to do about it?

<--- Score

227. What is your competitive advantage?

<--- Score

228. Is Predictive Analytics realistic, or are you setting yourself up for failure?
<--- Score

229. What would you recommend your friend do if he/she were facing this dilemma?
<--- Score

230. Are there any activities that you can take off your to do list?
<--- Score

231. How do you foster innovation?
<--- Score

232. When you map the key players in your own work and the types/domains of relationships with them, which relationships do you find easy and which challenging, and why?
<--- Score

233. Do you feel that more should be done in the Predictive Analytics area?
<--- Score

234. What you are going to do to affect the numbers?
<--- Score

235. What are the gaps in your knowledge and experience?
<--- Score

236. Did your employees make progress today?
<--- Score

237. How do you govern and fulfill your societal

responsibilities?

<--- Score

238. Which functions and people interact with the supplier and or customer?

<--- Score

239. How do you go about securing Predictive Analytics?

<--- Score

240. How do you cross-sell and up-sell your Predictive Analytics success?

<--- Score

241. Who uses your product in ways you never expected?

<--- Score

242. Were lessons learned captured and communicated?

<--- Score

243. Do you know what you are doing? And who do you call if you don't?

<--- Score

Add up total points for this section:

_ _ _ _ _ = Total points for this section

Divided by: _ _ _ _ _ _ (number of statements answered) = _ _ _ _ _ _
Average score for this section

Transfer your score to the Predictive Analytics Index at the beginning of the

Self-Assessment.

Predictive Analytics and Managing Projects, Criteria for Project Managers:

1.0 Initiating Process Group: Predictive Analytics

1. When must it be done?

2. What business situation is being addressed?

3. Based on your Predictive Analytics project communication management plan, what worked well?

4. How will it affect me?

5. What will be the pressing issues of tomorrow?

6. Are identified risks being monitored properly, are new risks arising during the Predictive Analytics project or are foreseen risks occurring?

7. What must be done?

8. How do you help others satisfy needs?

9. When are the deliverables to be generated in each phase?

10. Are you certain deliverables are properly completed and meet quality standards?

11. How can you make your needs known?

12. How to control and approve each phase?

13. What areas does the group agree are the biggest success on the Predictive Analytics project?

14. What is the NEXT thing to do?

15. How well did the chosen processes produce the expected results?

16. Realistic - are the desired results expressed in a way that the team will be motivated and believe that the required level of involvement will be obtained?

17. What will you do to minimize the impact should a risk event occur?

18. If action is called for, what form should it take?

19. Are stakeholders properly informed about the status of the Predictive Analytics project?

20. How is each deliverable reviewed, verified, and validated?

1.1 Project Charter: Predictive Analytics

21. What are you trying to accomplish?

22. Customer: who are you doing the Predictive Analytics project for?

23. If finished, on what date did it finish?

24. Name and describe the elements that deal with providing the detail?

25. Who is the sponsor?

26. Why executive support?

27. How much?

28. What date will the task finish?

29. Major high-level milestone targets: what events measure progress?

30. What is in it for you?

31. Run it as as a startup?

32. How are Predictive Analytics projects different from operations?

33. Who manages integration?

34. What is the justification?

35. What are the constraints?

36. Strategic fit: what is the strategic initiative identifier for this Predictive Analytics project?

37. Why Outsource?

38. What are the assumptions?

39. When do you use a Predictive Analytics project Charter?

40. Why do you manage integration?

1.2 Stakeholder Register: Predictive Analytics

41. What opportunities exist to provide communications?

42. How will reports be created?

43. Who are the stakeholders?

44. What are the major Predictive Analytics project milestones requiring communications or providing communications opportunities?

45. How should employers make voices heard?

46. What & Why?

47. Who wants to talk about Security?

48. Is your organization ready for change?

49. How big is the gap?

50. How much influence do they have on the Predictive Analytics project?

51. Who is managing stakeholder engagement?

52. What is the power of the stakeholder?

1.3 Stakeholder Analysis Matrix: Predictive Analytics

53. Vulnerable groups; who are the vulnerable groups that might be affected by the Predictive Analytics project?

54. Who influences whom?

55. Participatory approach: how will key stakeholders participate in the Predictive Analytics project?

56. Advantages of proposition?

57. What coalitions might build around the issues being tackled?

58. Has there been a similar initiative in the region?

59. Where are mitigation costs factored in?

60. If the baseline is now, and if its improved it will be better than now?

61. What do people from other organizations see as your organizations weaknesses?

62. Timescales, deadlines and pressures?

63. Gaps in capabilities?

64. Cashflow, start-up cash-drain?

65. Guiding question: what is the issue at stake?

66. How can you fill the need to show progress?

67. Would it be fair to say that cost is a controlling criteria?

68. Vital contracts and partners?

69. Which conditions out of the control of the management are crucial for the achievement of the immediate objective?

70. Could any of your organizations weaknesses seriously threaten development?

71. Disadvantages of proposition?

72. Competitor intentions - various?

2.0 Planning Process Group: Predictive Analytics

73. To what extent are the participating departments coordinating with each other?

74. Explanation: is what the Predictive Analytics project intents to solve a hard question?

75. How does activity resource estimation affect activity duration estimation?

76. To what extent do the intervention objectives and strategies of the Predictive Analytics project respond to your organizations plans?

77. What makes your Predictive Analytics project successful?

78. When developing the estimates for Predictive Analytics project phases, you choose to add the individual estimates for the activities that comprise each phase. What type of estimation method are you using?

79. What should you do next?

80. To what extent and in what ways are the Predictive Analytics project contributing to progress towards organizational reform?

81. What is the critical path for this Predictive Analytics project, and what is the duration of the

critical path?

82. Will you be replaced?

83. The Predictive Analytics project charter is created in which Predictive Analytics project management process group?

84. Predictive Analytics project assessment; why did you do this Predictive Analytics project?

85. How well did the chosen processes fit the needs of the Predictive Analytics project?

86. To what extent is the program helping to influence your organizations policy framework?

87. How well defined and documented are the Predictive Analytics project management processes you chose to use?

88. In which Predictive Analytics project management process group is the detailed Predictive Analytics project budget created?

89. If a task is partitionable, is this a sufficient condition to reduce the Predictive Analytics project duration?

90. Just how important is your work to the overall success of the Predictive Analytics project?

91. When will the Predictive Analytics project be done?

2.1 Project Management Plan: Predictive Analytics

92. What does management expect of PMs?

93. What did not work so well?

94. What is the business need?

95. What would you do differently?

96. Are alternatives safe, functional, constructible, economical, reasonable and sustainable?

97. Why Change?

98. How well are you able to manage your risk?

99. Are calculations and results of analyzes essentially correct?

100. Are there any client staffing expectations?

101. Is the budget realistic?

102. How do you manage integration?

103. Do there need to be organizational changes?

104. Who is the Predictive Analytics project Manager?

105. What are the training needs?

106. How do you manage time?

107. What went right?

108. What happened during the process that you found interesting?

109. What worked well?

2.2 Scope Management Plan: Predictive Analytics

110. Were Predictive Analytics project team members involved in the development of activity & task decomposition?

111. Has appropriate allowance been made for the effect of the learning curve on all personnel joining the Predictive Analytics project who do not have the required prior industry, functional & technical expertise?

112. Is there a requirements change management processes in place?

113. Are all resource assumptions documented?

114. Does the implementation plan have an appropriate division of responsibilities?

115. Materials available for performing the work?

116. Is there an onboarding process in place?

117. Is there an approved case?

118. Alignment to strategic goals & objectives?

119. The greatest degree of uncertainty is encountered during which phase of the Predictive Analytics project life cycle?

120. How are you planning to maintain the scope baseline and how will you manage scope changes?

121. What problem is being solved by delivering this Predictive Analytics project?

122. Is current scope of the Predictive Analytics project substantially different than that originally defined?

123. Has the selected plan been formulated using cost effectiveness and incremental analysis techniques?

124. Are the payment terms being followed?

125. Is there a formal process for updating the Predictive Analytics project baseline?

126. Are meeting minutes captured and sent out after the meeting?

127. Have Predictive Analytics project management standards and procedures been identified / established and documented?

128. Is there a formal set of procedures supporting Issues Management?

2.3 Requirements Management Plan: Predictive Analytics

129. Is requirements work dependent on any other specific Predictive Analytics project or non-Predictive Analytics project activities (e.g. funding, approvals, procurement)?

130. The wbs is developed as part of a joint planning session. and how do you know that youhave done this right?

131. Did you avoid subjective, flowery or non-specific statements?

132. What are you trying to do?

133. How will unresolved questions be handled once approval has been obtained?

134. How will the information be distributed?

135. Does the Predictive Analytics project have a Change Control process?

136. Will the Predictive Analytics project requirements become approved in writing?

137. Will you use tracing to help understand the impact of a change in requirements?

138. Is any organizational data being used or stored?

139. Who will initially review the Predictive Analytics project work or products to ensure it meets the applicable acceptance criteria?

140. Is the system software (non-operating system) new to the IT Predictive Analytics project team?

141. Did you distinguish the scope of work the contractor(s) will be required to do?

142. Could inaccurate or incomplete requirements in this Predictive Analytics project create a serious risk for the business?

143. Who will do the reporting and to whom will reports be delivered?

144. Do you have an agreed upon process for alerting the Predictive Analytics project Manager if a request for change in requirements leads to a product scope change?

145. Who will finally present the work or product(s) for acceptance?

146. Do you expect stakeholders to be cooperative?

147. Will you use an assessment of the Predictive Analytics project environment as a tool to discover risk to the requirements process?

148. How will the requirements become prioritized?

2.4 Requirements Documentation: Predictive Analytics

149. How will requirements be documented and who signs off on them?

150. What if the system wasn t implemented?

151. Do technical resources exist?

152. Is the origin of the requirement clearly stated?

153. Is the requirement properly understood?

154. Verifiability. can the requirements be checked?

155. Does your organization restrict technical alternatives?

156. Has requirements gathering uncovered information that would necessitate changes?

157. What facilities must be supported by the system?

158. Consistency. are there any requirements conflicts?

159. How much testing do you need to do to prove that your system is safe?

160. What kind of entity is a problem ?

161. How do you get the user to tell you what they

want?

162. What are the acceptance criteria?

163. How does the proposed Predictive Analytics project contribute to the overall objectives of your organization?

164. Is new technology needed?

165. The problem with gathering requirements is right there in the word gathering. What images does it conjure?

166. What is effective documentation?

167. What images does it conjure?

168. How to document system requirements?

2.5 Requirements Traceability Matrix: Predictive Analytics

169. Will you use a Requirements Traceability Matrix?

170. Why use a WBS?

171. What is the WBS?

172. How do you manage scope?

173. Describe the process for approving requirements so they can be added to the traceability matrix and Predictive Analytics project work can be performed. Will the Predictive Analytics project requirements become approved in writing?

174. How will it affect the stakeholders personally in their career?

175. What are the chronologies, contingencies, consequences, criteria?

176. What percentage of Predictive Analytics projects are producing traceability matrices between requirements and other work products?

177. Is there a requirements traceability process in place?

178. How small is small enough?

179. Do you have a clear understanding of all

subcontracts in place?

180. Why do you manage scope?

2.6 Project Scope Statement: Predictive Analytics

181. Elements of scope management that deal with concept development ?

182. Are there completion/verification criteria defined for each task producing an output?

183. Is the Predictive Analytics project manager qualified and experienced in Predictive Analytics project management?

184. Is the plan for Predictive Analytics project resources adequate?

185. What process would you recommend for creating the Predictive Analytics project scope statement?

186. If you were to write a list of what should not be included in the scope statement, what are the things that you would recommend be described as out-of-scope?

187. Has the Predictive Analytics project scope statement been reviewed as part of the baseline process?

188. Has everyone approved the Predictive Analytics projects scope statement?

189. Have you been able to thoroughly document the Predictive Analytics projects assumptions and

constraints?

190. Are the meetings set up to have assigned note takers that will add action/issues to the issue list?

191. Predictive Analytics project lead, team lead, solution architect?

192. Do you anticipate new stakeholders joining the Predictive Analytics project over time?

193. Will you need a statement of work?

194. Where and how does the team fit within your organization structure?

195. Will an issue form be in use?

196. Is the quality function identified and assigned?

197. What is a process you might recommend to verify the accuracy of the research deliverable?

198. What is change?

199. Is there a baseline plan against which to measure progress?

200. Why do you need to manage scope?

2.7 Assumption and Constraint Log: Predictive Analytics

201. No superfluous information or marketing narrative?

202. Is the definition of the Predictive Analytics project scope clear; what needs to be accomplished?

203. Have you eliminated all duplicative tasks or manual efforts, where appropriate?

204. What weaknesses do you have?

205. Is there documentation of system capability requirements, data requirements, environment requirements, security requirements, and computer and hardware requirements?

206. Would known impacts serve as impediments?

207. How many Predictive Analytics project staff does this specific process affect?

208. Does a specific action and/or state that is known to violate security policy occur?

209. Should factors be unpredictable over time?

210. Is the amount of effort justified by the anticipated value of forming a new process?

211. Is staff trained on the software technologies that

are being used on the Predictive Analytics project?

212. What other teams / processes would be impacted by changes to the current process, and how?

213. Does the document/deliverable meet all requirements (for example, statement of work) specific to this deliverable?

214. Do documented requirements exist for all critical components and areas, including technical, business, interfaces, performance, security and conversion requirements?

215. Do the requirements meet the standards of correctness, completeness, consistency, accuracy, and readability?

216. Have all involved stakeholders and work groups committed to the Predictive Analytics project?

217. After observing execution of process, is it in compliance with the documented Plan?

218. Is the process working, and people are not executing in compliance of the process?

219. Has a Predictive Analytics project Communications Plan been developed?

2.8 Work Breakdown Structure: Predictive Analytics

220. When would you develop a Work Breakdown Structure?

221. How many levels?

222. How much detail?

223. What has to be done?

224. When does it have to be done?

225. How far down?

226. Where does it take place?

227. How will you and your Predictive Analytics project team define the Predictive Analytics projects scope and work breakdown structure?

228. Is it a change in scope?

229. Who has to do it?

230. How big is a work-package?

231. Why is it useful?

232. Is it still viable?

233. What is the probability that the Predictive

Analytics project duration will exceed xx weeks?

234. Is the work breakdown structure (wbs) defined and is the scope of the Predictive Analytics project clear with assigned deliverable owners?

235. What is the probability of completing the Predictive Analytics project in less that xx days?

236. Can you make it?

237. Why would you develop a Work Breakdown Structure?

238. When do you stop?

239. Do you need another level?

2.9 WBS Dictionary: Predictive Analytics

240. Are the responsibilities and authorities of each of the above organizational elements or managers clearly defined?

241. Does the contractor have procedures which permit identification of recurring or non-recurring costs as necessary?

242. Wbs elements contractually specified for reporting of status to you (lowest level only)?

243. Are the rates for allocating costs from each indirect cost pool to contracts updated as necessary to ensure a realistic monthly allocation of indirect costs without significant year-end adjustments?

244. Are the bases and rates for allocating costs from each indirect pool to commercial work consistent with the already stated used to allocate corresponding costs to Government contracts?

245. The already stated responsible for overhead performance control of related costs?

246. All cwbs elements specified for external reporting?

247. Are the procedures for identifying indirect costs to incurring organizations, indirect cost pools, and allocating the costs from the pools to the contracts

formally documented?

248. Are significant decision points, constraints, and interfaces identified as key milestones?

249. What is the end result of a work package?

250. Are all affected work authorizations, budgeting, and scheduling documents amended to properly reflect the effects of authorized changes?

251. Are current work performance indicators and goals relatable to original goals as modified by contractual changes, replanning, and reprogramming actions?

252. Are records maintained to show how undistributed budgets are controlled?

253. Intermediate schedules, as required, which provide a logical sequence from the master schedule to the control account level?

254. Is each control account assigned to a single organizational element directly responsible for the work and identifiable to a single element of the CWBS?

255. Are meaningful indicators identified for use in measuring the status of cost and schedule performance?

2.10 Schedule Management Plan: Predictive Analytics

256. Have Predictive Analytics project management standards and procedures been identified / established and documented?

257. Are there any activities or deliverables being added or gold-plated that could be dropped or scaled back without falling short of the original requirement?

258. Has the Predictive Analytics project manager been identified?

259. Has a structured approach been used to break work effort into manageable components (WBS)?

260. Is a payment system in place with proper reviews and approvals?

261. What will be the final cost of the Predictive Analytics project if status quo is maintained?

262. Are the processes for schedule assessment and analysis defined?

263. Is current scope of the Predictive Analytics project substantially different than that originally defined?

264. Are mitigation strategies identified?

265. Time for overtime?

266. Are cause and effect determined for risks when they occur?

267. Have the procedures for identifying budget variances been followed?

268. Is the development plan and/or process documented?

269. Are Predictive Analytics project leaders committed to this Predictive Analytics project full time?

270. Were Predictive Analytics project team members involved in detailed estimating and scheduling?

271. Personnel with expertise?

272. Are Predictive Analytics project team members involved in detailed estimating and scheduling?

273. Does the Predictive Analytics project have a Statement of Work?

2.11 Activity List: Predictive Analytics

274. Who will perform the work?

275. When will the work be performed?

276. How difficult will it be to do specific activities on this Predictive Analytics project?

277. In what sequence?

278. What is the total time required to complete the Predictive Analytics project if no delays occur?

279. Is there anything planned that does not need to be here?

280. What are you counting on?

281. What will be performed?

282. How can the Predictive Analytics project be displayed graphically to better visualize the activities?

283. Are the required resources available or need to be acquired?

284. What went well?

285. How do you determine the late start (LS) for each activity?

286. What did not go as well?

287. Should you include sub-activities?

288. How should ongoing costs be monitored to try to keep the Predictive Analytics project within budget?

289. Is infrastructure setup part of your Predictive Analytics project?

290. For other activities, how much delay can be tolerated?

291. Can you determine the activity that must finish, before this activity can start?

2.12 Activity Attributes: Predictive Analytics

292. Do you feel very comfortable with your prediction?

293. What went wrong?

294. What is missing?

295. Would you consider either of corresponding activities an outlier?

296. Are the required resources available?

297. Resources to accomplish the work?

298. Which method produces the more accurate cost assignment?

299. Activity: fair or not fair?

300. What is the general pattern here?

301. How many days do you need to complete the work scope with a limit of X number of resources?

302. Is there a trend during the year?

303. Resource is assigned to?

304. Can you re-assign any activities to another resource to resolve an over-allocation?

305. How difficult will it be to complete specific activities on this Predictive Analytics project?

306. Were there other ways you could have organized the data to achieve similar results?

307. Activity: what is Missing?

308. Where else does it apply?

309. Why?

2.13 Milestone List: Predictive Analytics

310. New USPs?

311. How late can each activity be finished and started?

312. How will the milestone be verified?

313. Loss of key staff?

314. Sustaining internal capabilities?

315. Environmental effects?

316. What would happen if a delivery of material was one week late?

317. Which path is the critical path?

318. Insurmountable weaknesses?

319. What background experience, skills, and strengths does the team bring to your organization?

320. It is to be a narrative text providing the crucial aspects of your Predictive Analytics project proposal answering what, who, how, when and where?

321. Describe your organizations strengths and core competencies. What factors will make your organization succeed?

322. Describe the industry you are in and the market growth opportunities. What is the market for your technology, product or service?

323. Level of the Innovation?

324. Global influences?

325. Can you derive how soon can the whole Predictive Analytics project finish?

326. How will you get the word out to customers?

2.14 Network Diagram: Predictive Analytics

327. What controls the start and finish of a job?

328. Review the logical flow of the network diagram. Take a look at which activities you have first and then sequence the activities. Do they make sense?

329. What are the Key Success Factors?

330. Which type of network diagram allows you to depict four types of dependencies?

331. What must be completed before an activity can be started?

332. What are the tools?

333. What activity must be completed immediately before this activity can start?

334. Can you calculate the confidence level?

335. Why must you schedule milestones, such as reviews, throughout the Predictive Analytics project?

336. What are the Major Administrative Issues?

337. Will crashing x weeks return more in benefits than it costs?

338. Planning: who, how long, what to do?

339. Are the gantt chart and/or network diagram updated periodically and used to assess the overall Predictive Analytics project timetable?

340. Are you on time?

341. What is the probability of completing the Predictive Analytics project in less that xx days?

342. If x is long, what would be the completion time if you break x into two parallel parts of y weeks and z weeks?

343. What job or jobs could run concurrently?

344. What is the lowest cost to complete this Predictive Analytics project in xx weeks?

345. Where do you schedule uncertainty time?

346. How difficult will it be to do specific activities on this Predictive Analytics project?

2.15 Activity Resource Requirements: Predictive Analytics

347. What are constraints that you might find during the Human Resource Planning process?

348. Do you use tools like decomposition and rolling-wave planning to produce the activity list and other outputs?

349. Other support in specific areas?

350. Are there unresolved issues that need to be addressed?

351. How many signatures do you require on a check and does this match what is in your policy and procedures?

352. Which logical relationship does the PDM use most often?

353. Why do you do that?

354. Organizational Applicability?

355. What is the Work Plan Standard?

356. When does monitoring begin?

357. Anything else?

358. How do you handle petty cash?

2.16 Resource Breakdown Structure: Predictive Analytics

359. Which resources should be in the resource pool?

360. Changes based on input from stakeholders?

361. Who will use the system?

362. What can you do to improve productivity?

363. What is Predictive Analytics project communication management?

364. Who is allowed to see what data about which resources?

365. The list could probably go on, but, the thing that you would most like to know is, How long & How much?

366. Goals for the Predictive Analytics project. What is each stakeholders desired outcome for the Predictive Analytics project?

367. Who needs what information?

368. Any changes from stakeholders?

369. Which resource planning tool provides information on resource responsibility and accountability?

370. Who delivers the information?

371. What is your organizations history in doing similar activities?

372. What are the requirements for resource data?

373. Why do you do it?

374. Why is this important?

2.17 Activity Duration Estimates: Predictive Analytics

375. Why is outsourcing growing so rapidly?

376. Are contingency plans created to prepare for risk events to occur?

377. Why is there a growing trend in outsourcing, especially in the government?

378. Does a procedure exist to ensure the Predictive Analytics project work is completed in the appropriate sequence and on time?

379. Do you think many other organizations could apply this methodology, or does each organization need to create its own methodology?

380. Calculate the expected duration for an activity that has a most likely time of 3, a pessimistic time of 10, and a optimiztic time of 2?

381. How can others help Predictive Analytics project managers understand your organizational context for Predictive Analytics projects?

382. Explanation notice how many choices are half right?

383. Do scope statements include the Predictive Analytics project objectives and expected deliverables?

384. Does a process exist to identify Predictive Analytics project roles, responsibilities and reporting relationships?

385. What time management activity should you do NEXT?

386. See what went wrong?

387. Is a work breakdown structure created to organize and to confirm the scope of each Predictive Analytics project?

388. Which best describes how this affects the Predictive Analytics project?

389. Are measurement techniques employed to determine the potential impact of proposed changes?

390. If Predictive Analytics project time and cost are not as important as the number of resources used each month, which is the BEST thing to do?

391. When a risk event occurs, is the risk response evaluated and the appropriate response implemented?

392. What is the BEST thing to do?

393. Will the new application negatively affect the current IT infrastructure?

2.18 Duration Estimating Worksheet: Predictive Analytics

394. How should ongoing costs be monitored to try to keep the Predictive Analytics project within budget?

395. How can the Predictive Analytics project be displayed graphically to better visualize the activities?

396. Do any colleagues have experience with your organization and/or RFPs?

397. Small or large Predictive Analytics project?

398. Can the Predictive Analytics project be constructed as planned?

399. What questions do you have?

400. Is the Predictive Analytics project responsive to community need?

401. What utility impacts are there?

402. What is the total time required to complete the Predictive Analytics project if no delays occur?

403. What are the critical bottleneck activities?

404. Value pocket identification & quantification what are value pockets?

405. What is an Average Predictive Analytics project?

406. Why estimate time and cost?

407. Done before proceeding with this activity or what can be done concurrently?

408. What info is needed?

409. When do the individual activities need to start and finish?

410. Does the Predictive Analytics project provide innovative ways for stakeholders to overcome obstacles or deliver better outcomes?

2.19 Project Schedule: Predictive Analytics

411. How does a Predictive Analytics project get to be a year late ?

412. Predictive Analytics project work estimates Who is managing the work estimate quality of work tasks in the Predictive Analytics project schedule?

413. Is infrastructure setup part of your Predictive Analytics project?

414. What is risk management?

415. How can you address that situation?

416. Why do you need schedules?

417. What is the difference?

418. Why is this particularly bad?

419. Change management required?

420. What is Predictive Analytics project management?

421. Is the structure for tracking the Predictive Analytics project schedule well defined and assigned to a specific individual?

422. How can slack be negative?

423. Why do you need to manage Predictive Analytics project Risk?

424. How much slack is available in the Predictive Analytics project?

425. Are procedures defined by which the Predictive Analytics project schedule may be changed?

426. If there are any qualifying green components to this Predictive Analytics project, what portion of the total Predictive Analytics project cost is green?

427. Eliminate unnecessary activities. Are there activities that came from a template or previous Predictive Analytics project that are not applicable on this phase of this Predictive Analytics project?

428. Why do you think schedule issues often cause the most conflicts on Predictive Analytics projects?

429. Meet requirements?

430. Understand the constraints used in preparing the schedule. Are activities connected because logic dictates the order in which others occur?

2.20 Cost Management Plan: Predictive Analytics

431. Have all documents been archived in a Predictive Analytics project repository for each release?

432. Have all team members been part of identifying risks?

433. Schedule contingency – how will the schedule contingency be administrated?

434. Are updated Predictive Analytics project time & resource estimates reasonable based on the current Predictive Analytics project stage?

435. Are changes in scope (deliverable commitments) agreed to by all affected groups & individuals?

436. Are action items captured and managed?

437. Does a documented Predictive Analytics project organizational policy & plan (i.e. governance model) exist?

438. Is pert / critical path or equivalent methodology being used?

439. Are trade-offs between accepting the risk and mitigating the risk identified?

440. Why do you manage cost?

441. Has the scope management document been updated and distributed to help prevent scope creep?

442. Contracting method – what contracting method is to be used for the contracts?

443. Is there any form of automated support for Issues Management?

444. Are Predictive Analytics project team members committed fulltime?

445. Are metrics used to evaluate and manage Vendors?

446. What is your organizations history in doing similar tasks?

447. Schedule preparation – how will the schedules be prepared during each phase of the Predictive Analytics project?

448. Is an industry recognized mechanized support tool(s) being used for Predictive Analytics project scheduling & tracking?

449. How difficult will it be to do specific tasks on the Predictive Analytics project?

450. Similar Predictive Analytics projects?

2.21 Activity Cost Estimates: Predictive Analytics

451. What are the audit requirements?

452. Eac -estimate at completion, what is the total job expected to cost?

453. Padding is bad and contingencies are good. what is the difference?

454. Certification of actual expenditures?

455. One way to define activities is to consider how organization employees describe jobs to families and friends. You basically want to know, What do you do?

456. Estimated cost?

457. Will you need to provide essential services information about activities?

458. What is a Predictive Analytics project Management Plan?

459. Who determines the quality and expertise of contractors?

460. In which phase of the acquisition process cycle does source qualifications reside?

461. Does the activity rely on a common set of tools to carry it out?

462. Who determines when the contractor is paid?

463. How many activities should you have?

464. What is procurement?

465. What is the activity inventory?

466. What defines a successful Predictive Analytics project?

467. The impact and what actions were taken?

468. How difficult will it be to do specific tasks on the Predictive Analytics project?

469. Were decisions made in a timely manner?

470. Was the consultant knowledgeable about the program?

2.22 Cost Estimating Worksheet: Predictive Analytics

471. What happens to any remaining funds not used?

472. What additional Predictive Analytics project(s) could be initiated as a result of this Predictive Analytics project?

473. What will others want?

474. What is the estimated labor cost today based upon this information?

475. Will the Predictive Analytics project collaborate with the local community and leverage resources?

476. Does the Predictive Analytics project provide innovative ways for stakeholders to overcome obstacles or deliver better outcomes?

477. Is it feasible to establish a control group arrangement?

478. How will the results be shared and to whom?

479. Identify the timeframe necessary to monitor progress and collect data to determine how the selected measure has changed?

480. Ask: are others positioned to know, are others credible, and will others cooperate?

481. Is the Predictive Analytics project responsive to community need?

482. What costs are to be estimated?

483. Can a trend be established from historical performance data on the selected measure and are the criteria for using trend analysis or forecasting methods met?

484. Who is best positioned to know and assist in identifying corresponding factors?

485. What can be included?

486. What is the purpose of estimating?

2.23 Cost Baseline: Predictive Analytics

487. Have all approved changes to the Predictive Analytics project requirement been identified and impact on the performance, cost, and schedule baselines documented?

488. Review your risk triggers -have your risks changed?

489. What is the consequence?

490. What threats might prevent you from getting there?

491. Has training and knowledge transfer of the operations organization been completed?

492. Have all the product or service deliverables been accepted by the customer?

493. On budget?

494. How do you manage cost?

495. Does it impact schedule, cost, quality?

496. For what purpose ?

497. Vac -variance at completion, how much over/ under budget do you expect to be?

498. Escalation criteria met?

499. When should cost estimates be developed?

500. What is it ?

501. What does a good WBS NOT look like?

502. Does a process exist for establishing a cost baseline to measure Predictive Analytics project performance?

503. Has the Predictive Analytics project documentation been archived or otherwise disposed as described in the Predictive Analytics project communication plan?

504. How concrete were original objectives?

505. Has the appropriate access to relevant data and analysis capability been granted?

2.24 Quality Management Plan: Predictive Analytics

506. Contradictory information between different documents?

507. How are people conducting sampling trained?

508. What is quality and how will you ensure it?

509. How does your organization establish and maintain customer relationships?

510. With the five whys method, the team considers why the issue being explored occurred. do others then take that initial answer and ask why?

511. Have Predictive Analytics project management standards and procedures been established and documented?

512. Results Available?

513. Were there any deficiencies / issues identified in the prior years self-assessment?

514. What is the Difference Between a QMP and QAPP?

515. Where do you focus?

516. What does it do for you (or to me)?

517. How does your organization use comparative data and information to improve organizational performance?

518. Documented results available?

519. What is quality planning ?

520. What is your organizations strategic planning process?

521. List your organizations customer contact standards that employees are expected to maintain. How are corresponding standards measured?

522. Are best practices and metrics employed to identify issues, progress, performance, etc.?

523. Meet how often?

524. What would you gain if you spent time working to improve this process?

525. Are there trends or hot spots?

2.25 Quality Metrics: Predictive Analytics

526. Is there a set of procedures to capture, analyze and act on quality metrics?

527. How should customers provide input?

528. Subjective quality component: customer satisfaction, how do you measure it?

529. How does one achieve stability?

530. Have alternatives been defined in the event that failure occurs?

531. How exactly do you define when differences exist?

532. Where is quality now?

533. Is quality culture a competitive advantage?

534. What do you measure?

535. Are applicable standards referenced and available?

536. What does this tell us?

537. Has trace of defects been initiated?

538. What metrics are important and most beneficial

to measure?

539. How do you measure?

540. The metrics–what is being considered?

541. Who is willing to lead?

542. Are quality metrics defined?

543. How can the effectiveness of each of the activities be measured?

544. What if the biggest risk to your business were the already stated people who do not complain?

545. Can visual measures help you to filter visualizations of interest?

2.26 Process Improvement Plan: Predictive Analytics

546. Have storage and access mechanisms and procedures been determined?

547. Are there forms and procedures to collect and record the data?

548. To elicit goal statements, do you ask a question such as, What do you want to achieve?

549. Are you meeting the quality standards?

550. Has a process guide to collect the data been developed?

551. Are you following the quality standards?

552. Purpose of goal: the motive is determined by asking, why do you want to achieve this goal?

553. What is the return on investment?

554. Have the frequency of collection and the points in the process where measurements will be made been determined?

555. Who should prepare the process improvement action plan?

556. Does explicit definition of the measures exist?

557. What makes people good SPI coaches?

558. Where are you now?

559. Everyone agrees on what process improvement is, right?

560. Why do you want to achieve the goal?

561. What personnel are the change agents for your initiative?

562. Are you making progress on the improvement framework?

563. What is the test-cycle concept?

564. Where do you want to be?

2.27 Responsibility Assignment Matrix: Predictive Analytics

565. Does the Predictive Analytics project need to be analyzed further to uncover additional responsibilities?

566. Why cost benefit analysis?

567. What do people write/say on status/Predictive Analytics project reports?

568. Actual cost of work performed?

569. Identify and isolate causes of favorable and unfavorable cost and schedule variances?

570. Budgeted cost for work performed?

571. Are records maintained to show how management reserves are used?

572. Are authorized changes being incorporated in a timely manner?

573. What tool can show you individual and group allocations?

574. Which Predictive Analytics project management knowledge area is least mature?

575. Evaluate the impact of schedule changes, work around, etc?

576. Does each role with Accountable responsibility have the authority within your organization to make the required decisions?

577. Changes in the nature of the overhead requirements?

578. The staff characteristics – is the group or the person capable to work together as a team?

579. Is it safe to say you can handle more work or that some tasks you are supposed to do arent worth doing?

580. How do you assist them to be as productive as possible?

581. Changes in the overhead pool and/or organization structures?

582. Is the entire contract planned in time-phased control accounts to the extent practicable?

583. Are indirect costs charged to the appropriate indirect pools and incurring organization?

584. What expertise is available in your department?

2.28 Roles and Responsibilities: Predictive Analytics

585. What is working well within your organizations performance management system?

586. Accountabilities: what are the roles and responsibilities of individual team members?

587. To decide whether to use a quality measurement, ask how will you know when it is achieved?

588. Are your policies supportive of a culture of quality data?

589. Where are you most strong as a supervisor?

590. Is there a training program in place for stakeholders covering expectations, roles and responsibilities and any addition knowledge others need to be good stakeholders?

591. Are Predictive Analytics project team roles and responsibilities identified and documented?

592. Implementation of actions: Who are the responsible units?

593. What should you do now to ensure that you are meeting all expectations of your current position?

594. What are your major roles and responsibilities in the area of performance measurement and

assessment?

595. Does your vision/mission support a culture of quality data?

596. Was the expectation clearly communicated?

597. Are Predictive Analytics project team roles and responsibilities identified and documented?

598. Does the team have access to and ability to use data analysis tools?

599. What should you highlight for improvement?

600. Be specific; avoid generalities. Thank you and great work alone are insufficient. What exactly do you appreciate and why?

601. Are your budgets supportive of a culture of quality data?

602. What specific behaviors did you observe?

603. Are governance roles and responsibilities documented?

604. Authority: what areas/Predictive Analytics projects in your work do you have the authority to decide upon and act on the already stated decisions?

2.29 Human Resource Management Plan: Predictive Analytics

605. Are tasks tracked by hours?

606. Measurable - are the targets measurable?

607. Has your organization readiness assessment been conducted?

608. Are enough systems & user personnel assigned to the Predictive Analytics project?

609. Are Predictive Analytics project team roles and responsibilities identified and documented?

610. Who is involved?

611. Have lessons learned been conducted after each Predictive Analytics project release?

612. Is there a Quality Management Plan?

613. How are superior performers differentiated from average performers?

614. Was the scope definition used in task sequencing?

615. Has the Predictive Analytics project manager been identified?

616. Are decisions captured in a decisions log?

617. How are you going to ensure that you have a well motivated workforce?

618. Is there general agreement & acceptance of the current status and progress of the Predictive Analytics project?

619. Are there checklists created to determine if all quality processes are followed?

620. Is the current culture aligned with the vision, mission, and values of the department?

621. Are Predictive Analytics project team members committed fulltime?

622. How do you determine what key skills and talents are needed to meet the objectives. Is your organization primarily focused on a specific industry?

623. Were the budget estimates reasonable?

624. Are milestone deliverables effectively tracked and compared to Predictive Analytics project plan?

2.30 Communications Management Plan: Predictive Analytics

625. Timing: when do the effects of the communication take place?

626. Can you think of other people who might have concerns or interests?

627. Is there an important stakeholder who is actively opposed and will not receive messages?

628. Which team member will work with each stakeholder?

629. Who is involved as you identify stakeholders?

630. What help do you and your team need from the stakeholder?

631. What is the stakeholders level of authority?

632. Who have you worked with in past, similar initiatives?

633. What is Predictive Analytics project communications management?

634. Where do team members get information?

635. Are there potential barriers between the team and the stakeholder?

636. What to learn?

637. How did the term stakeholder originate?

638. Who did you turn to if you had questions?

639. Which stakeholders can influence others?

640. In your work, how much time is spent on stakeholder identification?

641. Why do you manage communications?

642. Who needs to know and how much?

643. Do you then often overlook a key stakeholder or stakeholder group?

644. Are you constantly rushing from meeting to meeting?

2.31 Risk Management Plan: Predictive Analytics

645. Methodology: how will risk management be performed on this Predictive Analytics project?

646. Risk may be made during which step of risk management?

647. Management -what contingency plans do you have if the risk becomes a reality?

648. Premium on reliability of product?

649. Has something like this been done before?

650. Do you manage the process through use of metrics?

651. Risk documentation: what reporting formats and processes will be used for risk management activities?

652. Are the best people available?

653. Do the requirements require the creation of components that are unlike anything your organization has previously built?

654. Are staff committed for the duration of the product?

655. Number of users of the product?

656. Is the customer willing to commit significant time to the requirements gathering process?

657. Who has experience with this?

658. Are testing tools available and suitable?

659. Do you train all developers in the process?

660. Technology risk: is the Predictive Analytics project technically feasible?

661. What is the cost to the Predictive Analytics project if it does occur?

662. Are there alternative opinions/solutions/ processes you should explore?

2.32 Risk Register: Predictive Analytics

663. What are you going to do to limit the Predictive Analytics projects risk exposure due to the identified risks?

664. Financial risk -can your organization afford to undertake the Predictive Analytics project?

665. How are risks identified?

666. Contingency actions - planned actions to reduce the immediate seriousness of the risk when it does occur. What should you do when?

667. Risk probability and impact: how will the probabilities and impacts of risk items be assessed?

668. What further options might be available for responding to the risk?

669. Schedule impact/severity estimated range (workdays) assume the event happens, what is the potential impact?

670. When would you develop a risk register?

671. When will it happen?

672. Assume the event happens, what is the Most Likely impact?

673. Do you require further engagement?

674. How often will the Risk Management Plan and Risk Register be formally reviewed, and by whom?

675. What would the impact to the Predictive Analytics project objectives be should the risk arise?

676. Assume the risk event or situation happens, what would the impact be?

677. People risk -are people with appropriate skills available to help complete the Predictive Analytics project?

678. Why would you develop a risk register?

679. How are risks graded?

680. What may happen or not go according to plan?

681. Are your objectives at risk?

682. When is it going to be done?

2.33 Probability and Impact Assessment: Predictive Analytics

683. Who will be in command to monitor and control the performance of the consortium members (consortium leader/client)?

684. How risk averse are you?

685. What risks are necessary to achieve success?

686. Do end-users have realistic expectations?

687. Is the technology to be built new to your organization?

688. Monitoring of the overall Predictive Analytics project status – are there any changes in the Predictive Analytics project that can effect and cause new possible risks?

689. Are the risk data timely and relevant?

690. Can you stabilize dynamic risk factors?

691. Are there new risks that mitigation strategies might introduce?

692. How solid is the Predictive Analytics projection of competitive reaction?

693. Do requirements put excessive performance constraints on the product?

694. Are tools for analysis and design available?

695. Which of your Predictive Analytics projects should be selected when compared with other Predictive Analytics projects?

696. What will be the likely political situation during the life of the Predictive Analytics project?

697. Do you have a mechanism for managing change?

698. What are the chances the risk event will occur?

699. Does the software engineering team have the right mix of skills?

700. Are team members trained in the use of the tools?

701. Workarounds are determined during which step of risk management?

2.34 Probability and Impact Matrix: Predictive Analytics

702. What can possibly go wrong?

703. Which role do you have in the Predictive Analytics project?

704. What kind of preparation would be required to do this?

705. Do requirements demand the use of new analysis, design, or testing methods?

706. Why do you need to manage Predictive Analytics project Risk?

707. What is the likelihood?

708. Are you working on the right risks?

709. Is Predictive Analytics project scope stable?

710. Have customers been involved fully in the definition of requirements?

711. Which of your Predictive Analytics projects should be selected when compared with other Predictive Analytics projects?

712. Prioritized components/features?

713. During Predictive Analytics project executing, a

team member identifies a risk that is not in the risk register. What should you do?

714. Several experts are offsite, and wish to be included. How can this be done?

715. What will be the likely political environment during the life of the Predictive Analytics project?

716. Were there any Predictive Analytics projects similar to this one in existence?

717. How are the local factors going to affect the absorption?

2.35 Risk Data Sheet: Predictive Analytics

718. What do people affected think about the need for, and practicality of preventive measures?

719. What actions can be taken to eliminate or remove risk?

720. Has a sensitivity analysis been carried out?

721. Whom do you serve (customers)?

722. What if client refuses?

723. What is the chance that it will happen?

724. Has the most cost-effective solution been chosen?

725. What are the main opportunities available to you that you should grab while you can?

726. If it happens, what are the consequences?

727. What was measured?

728. What are you weak at and therefore need to do better?

729. How can hazards be reduced?

730. Do effective diagnostic tests exist?

731. Potential for recurrence?

732. Will revised controls lead to tolerable risk levels?

733. What do you know?

734. What can happen?

735. What will be the consequences if it happens?

736. What is the environment within which you operate (social trends, economic, community values, broad based participation, national directions etc.)?

737. Type of risk identified?

2.36 Procurement Management Plan: Predictive Analytics

738. Is an industry recognized mechanized support tool(s) being used for Predictive Analytics project scheduling & tracking?

739. What were things that you did very well and want to do the same again on the next Predictive Analytics project?

740. Is the assigned Predictive Analytics project manager a PMP (Certified Predictive Analytics project manager) and experienced?

741. Are corrective actions and variances reported?

742. Are the budget estimates reasonable?

743. Is the Predictive Analytics project schedule available for all Predictive Analytics project team members to review?

744. Has Predictive Analytics project success criteria been defined?

745. Are Predictive Analytics project team members committed fulltime?

746. Have the key elements of a coherent Predictive Analytics project management strategy been established?

747. Are quality inspections and review activities listed in the Predictive Analytics project schedule(s)?

748. How will the duration of the Predictive Analytics project influence your decisions?

749. Do all stakeholders know how to access the PM repository and where to find the Predictive Analytics project documentation?

750. Are assumptions being identified, recorded, analyzed, qualified and closed?

751. Were escalated issues resolved promptly?

752. Are issues raised, assessed, actioned, and resolved in a timely and efficient manner?

753. Are the Predictive Analytics project team members located locally to the users/stakeholders?

754. Was the Predictive Analytics project schedule reviewed by all stakeholders and formally accepted?

2.37 Source Selection Criteria: Predictive Analytics

755. Does your documentation identify why the team concurs or differs with reported performance from past performance report (CPARs, questionnaire responses, etc.)?

756. How do you facilitate evaluation against published criteria?

757. What are the steps in performing a cost/tech tradeoff?

758. What common questions or problems are associated with debriefings?

759. How should oral presentations be prepared for?

760. What should be the contracting officers strategy?

761. What benefits are accrued from issuing a DRFP in advance of issuing a final RFP?

762. What is the last item a Predictive Analytics project manager must do to finalize Predictive Analytics project close-out?

763. Who is on the Source Selection Advisory Committee?

764. In order of importance, which evaluation criteria are the most critical to the determination of your

overall rating?

765. What is the basis of an estimate and what assumptions were made?

766. What will you use to capture evaluation and subsequent documentation?

767. When and what information can be considered with offerors regarding past performance?

768. Are they compliant with all technical requirements?

769. Are types/quantities of material, facilities appropriate?

770. How should the oral presentations be handled?

771. Does an evaluation need to include the identification of strengths and weaknesses?

772. What are the limitations on pre-competitive range communications?

773. Do you want to have them collaborate at subfactor level?

774. When is it appropriate to conduct a preproposal conference?

2.38 Stakeholder Management Plan: Predictive Analytics

775. Is the quality assurance team identified?

776. Are all vendor contracts closed out?

777. Are schedule deliverables actually delivered?

778. Has the Predictive Analytics project manager been identified?

779. What process was used to identify risks to the Predictive Analytics projects success?

780. Does the Predictive Analytics project have a formal Predictive Analytics project Charter?

781. Is a pmo (Predictive Analytics project management office) in place and does it provide oversight to the Predictive Analytics project?

782. Is the communication plan being followed?

783. Where are the verification requirements to be documented (eg purchase order, agreement etc)?

784. Are communication systems proposed compatible with staff skills and experience?

785. What is the general purpose in defining responsibilities of the already stated affiliated with the Predictive Analytics project?

786. Can you perform this task or activity in a more effective manner?

787. What is to be the method of release?

788. Does the detailed work plan match the complexity of tasks with the capabilities of personnel?

789. Is it standard practice to formally commit stakeholders to the Predictive Analytics project via agreements?

790. Does the role of the Predictive Analytics project Team cease upon the delivery of the Predictive Analytics projects outputs?

791. Is the performance of the supplier to be rated and documented?

792. When would you develop a Predictive Analytics project Execution Plan?

2.39 Change Management Plan: Predictive Analytics

793. Has the relevant business unit been notified of installation and support requirements?

794. Will a different work structure focus people on what is important?

795. What prerequisite knowledge or training is required?

796. What relationships will change?

797. Who in the business it includes?

798. Has the training provider been established?

799. Have the systems been configured and tested?

800. Different application of an existing process?

801. What provokes organizational change?

802. What risks may occur upfront, during implementation and after implementation?

803. What do you expect the target audience to do, say, think or feel as a result of this communication?

804. What method and medium would you use to announce a message?

805. What are the training strategies?

806. What new behaviours are required?

807. Have the business unit contacts been selected and notified?

808. What new roles are needed?

809. What are the dependencies?

810. Will the readiness criteria be met prior to the training roll out?

811. Do there need to be new channels developed?

812. What is the worst thing that can happen if you communicate information?

3.0 Executing Process Group: Predictive Analytics

813. Do the products created live up to the necessary quality?

814. It under budget or over budget?

815. How will you avoid scope creep?

816. What good practices or successful experiences or transferable examples have been identified?

817. On which process should team members spend the most time?

818. Does the Predictive Analytics project team have enough people to execute the Predictive Analytics project plan?

819. How do you prevent staff are just doing busywork to pass the time?

820. How could you control progress of your Predictive Analytics project?

821. What is the difference between conceptual, application, and evaluative questions?

822. Is the schedule for the set products being met?

823. How will professionals learn what is expected from them what the deliverables are?

824. What areas does the group agree are the biggest success on the Predictive Analytics project?

825. What does it mean to take a systems view of a Predictive Analytics project?

826. When do you share the scorecard with managers?

827. When is the appropriate time to bring the scorecard to Board meetings?

828. Mitigate. what will you do to minimize the impact should a risk event occur?

829. How does a Predictive Analytics project life cycle differ from a product life cycle?

830. Do your results resemble a normal distribution?

831. If a risk event occurs, what will you do?

832. What are crucial elements of successful Predictive Analytics project plan execution?

3.1 Team Member Status Report: Predictive Analytics

833. Why is it to be done?

834. Does your organization have the means (staff, money, contract, etc.) to produce or to acquire the product, good, or service?

835. The problem with Reward & Recognition Programs is that the truly deserving people all too often get left out. How can you make it practical?

836. How will resource planning be done?

837. Does every department have to have a Predictive Analytics project Manager on staff?

838. How it is to be done?

839. When a teams productivity and success depend on collaboration and the efficient flow of information, what generally fails them?

840. Does the product, good, or service already exist within your organization?

841. Do you have an Enterprise Predictive Analytics project Management Office (EPMO)?

842. How can you make it practical?

843. How does this product, good, or service meet

the needs of the Predictive Analytics project and your organization as a whole?

844. Are the products of your organizations Predictive Analytics projects meeting customers objectives?

845. What specific interest groups do you have in place?

846. How much risk is involved?

847. What is to be done?

848. Are the attitudes of staff regarding Predictive Analytics project work improving?

849. Will the staff do training or is that done by a third party?

850. Are your organizations Predictive Analytics projects more successful over time?

851. Is there evidence that staff is taking a more professional approach toward management of your organizations Predictive Analytics projects?

3.2 Change Request: Predictive Analytics

852. Who is communicating the change?

853. Will all change requests be unconditionally tracked through this process?

854. When to submit a change request?

855. Which requirements attributes affect the risk to reliability the most?

856. Change request coordination ?

857. Who needs to approve change requests?

858. What are the duties of the change control team?

859. What should be regulated in a change control operating instruction?

860. What kind of information about the change request needs to be captured?

861. Have scm procedures for noting the change, recording it, and reporting it been followed?

862. Are there requirements attributes that are strongly related to the complexity and size?

863. Has a formal technical review been conducted to assess technical correctness?

864. What are the basic mechanics of the Change Advisory Board (CAB)?

865. For which areas does this operating procedure apply?

866. Has your address changed?

867. How does your organization control changes before and after software is released to a customer?

868. How well do experienced software developers predict software change?

869. Has the change been highlighted and documented in the CSCI?

870. What is the function of the change control committee?

871. What can be filed?

3.3 Change Log: Predictive Analytics

872. Is the submitted change a new change or a modification of a previously approved change?

873. Is the change backward compatible without limitations?

874. Does the suggested change request seem to represent a necessary enhancement to the product?

875. Does the suggested change request represent a desired enhancement to the products functionality?

876. How does this change affect the timeline of the schedule?

877. How does this relate to the standards developed for specific business processes?

878. Do the described changes impact on the integrity or security of the system?

879. Is the requested change request a result of changes in other Predictive Analytics project(s)?

880. When was the request submitted?

881. How does this change affect scope?

882. Is this a mandatory replacement?

883. Is the change request within Predictive Analytics project scope?

884. Who initiated the change request?

885. Should a more thorough impact analysis be conducted?

886. When was the request approved?

887. Where do changes come from?

888. Will the Predictive Analytics project fail if the change request is not executed?

889. Is the change request open, closed or pending?

3.4 Decision Log: Predictive Analytics

890. Is everything working as expected?

891. How do you define success?

892. Does anything need to be adjusted?

893. How does the use a Decision Support System influence the strategies/tactics or costs?

894. What makes you different or better than others companies selling the same thing?

895. Is your opponent open to a non-traditional workflow, or will it likely challenge anything you do?

896. What eDiscovery problem or issue did your organization set out to fix or make better?

897. Who is the decisionmaker?

898. At what point in time does loss become unacceptable?

899. Who will be given a copy of this document and where will it be kept?

900. What alternatives/risks were considered?

901. How effective is maintaining the log at facilitating organizational learning?

902. Do strategies and tactics aimed at less than full

control reduce the costs of management or simply shift the cost burden?

903. How does an increasing emphasis on cost containment influence the strategies and tactics used?

904. Decision-making process; how will the team make decisions?

905. What was the rationale for the decision?

906. Meeting purpose; why does this team meet?

907. What is the average size of your matters in an applicable measurement?

908. How consolidated and comprehensive a story can you tell by capturing currently available incident data in a central location and through a log of key decisions during an incident?

909. Which variables make a critical difference?

3.5 Quality Audit: Predictive Analytics

910. Are all employees including salespersons made aware that they must report all complaints received from any source for inclusion in the complaint handling system?

911. Do all staff have the necessary authority and resources to deliver what is expected of them?

912. Are the policies and processes, as set out in the Quality Audit Manual, properly applied?

913. How does your organization know that its relationship with its (past) staff is appropriately effective and constructive?

914. Are all staff empowered and encouraged to contribute to ongoing improvement efforts?

915. How does your organization know that its relationships with industry and employers are appropriately effective and constructive?

916. Has a written procedure been established to identify devices during all stages of receipt, reconditioning, distribution and installation so that mix-ups are prevented?

917. What experience do staff have in the type of work that the audit entails?

918. Are complaint files maintained?

919. How does your organization know that its Mission, Vision and Values Statements are appropriate and effectively guiding your organization?

920. How does your organization know that the support for its staff is appropriately effective and constructive?

921. How does your organization know that its information technology system is serving its needs as effectively and constructively as is appropriate?

922. Are salvageable and salvaged medical devices stored in a manner to prevent damage and/or contamination?

923. Is there a written procedure for receiving materials?

924. How does your organization know that its system for supporting staff research capability is appropriately effective and constructive?

925. How does your organization know that its teaching activities (and staff learning) are effectively and constructively enhanced by its activities?

926. How does your organization know that its security arrangements are appropriately effective and constructive?

927. How does your organization know that its methods are appropriately effective and constructive?

928. How does your organization know that its staff have appropriate access to a fair and effective

grievance process?

929. Quality is about improvement and accountability. The immediate questions that arise out of that statement are: (i) improvement on what, and (ii) accountable to whom?

3.6 Team Directory: Predictive Analytics

930. Is construction on schedule?

931. How does the team resolve conflicts and ensure tasks are completed?

932. Does a Predictive Analytics project team directory list all resources assigned to the Predictive Analytics project?

933. Who will write the meeting minutes and distribute?

934. Have you decided when to celebrate the Predictive Analytics projects completion date?

935. Who will report Predictive Analytics project status to all stakeholders?

936. Who are your stakeholders (customers, sponsors, end users, team members)?

937. Timing: when do the effects of communication take place?

938. When will you produce deliverables?

939. Decisions: what could be done better to improve the quality of the constructed product?

940. Where should the information be distributed?

941. Process decisions: which organizational elements and which individuals will be assigned management functions?

942. Why is the work necessary?

943. Process decisions: are all start-up, turn over and close out requirements of the contract satisfied?

944. Days from the time the issue is identified?

945. How will the team handle changes?

946. Do purchase specifications and configurations match requirements?

947. Who are the Team Members?

948. How do unidentified risks impact the outcome of the Predictive Analytics project?

949. Decisions: is the most suitable form of contract being used?

3.7 Team Operating Agreement: Predictive Analytics

950. Are there more than two functional areas represented by your team?

951. Seconds for members to respond?

952. What types of accommodations will be formulated and put in place for sustaining the team?

953. Are there the right people on your team?

954. What is the anticipated procedure (recruitment, solicitation of volunteers, or assignment) for selecting team members?

955. What individual strengths does each team member bring to the group?

956. Are leadership responsibilities shared among team members (versus a single leader)?

957. Are there more than two national cultures represented by your team?

958. To whom do you deliver your services?

959. Confidentiality: how will confidential information be handled?

960. Do you post any action items, due dates, and responsibilities on the team website?

961. Conflict resolution: how will disputes and other conflicts be mediated or resolved?

962. Do you leverage technology engagement tools group chat, polls, screen sharing, etc.?

963. What is culture?

964. Do you vary your voice pace, tone and pitch to engage participants and gain involvement?

965. Do you determine the meeting length and time of day?

966. What is a Virtual Team?

967. Are there differences in access to communication and collaboration technology based on team member location?

968. Did you recap the meeting purpose, time, and expectations?

3.8 Team Performance Assessment: Predictive Analytics

969. Does more radicalness mean more perceived benefits?

970. To what degree are staff involved as partners in the improvement process?

971. To what degree will new and supplemental skills be introduced as the need is recognized?

972. To what degree do members articulate the goals beyond the team membership?

973. What are you doing specifically to develop the leaders around you?

974. To what degree do team members agree with the goals, relative importance, and the ways in which achievement will be measured?

975. To what degree do team members frequently explore the teams purpose and its implications?

976. If you are worried about method variance before you collect data, what sort of design elements might you include to reduce or eliminate the threat of method variance?

977. How does Predictive Analytics project termination impact Predictive Analytics project team members?

978. To what degree are the goals realistic?

979. To what degree does the teams approach to its work allow for modification and improvement over time?

980. To what degree is the team cognizant of small wins to be celebrated along the way?

981. Is there a particular method of data analysis that you would recommend as a means of demonstrating that method variance is not of great concern for a given dataset?

982. To what degree are the goals ambitious?

983. Individual task proficiency and team process behavior: what is important for team functioning?

984. To what degree are the skill areas critical to team performance present?

985. Where to from here?

986. Do friends perform better than acquaintances?

987. How do you recognize and praise members for contributions?

988. If you have criticized someones work for method variance in your role as reviewer, what was the circumstance?

3.9 Team Member Performance Assessment: Predictive Analytics

989. How do you make use of research?

990. What qualities does a successful Team leader possess?

991. What are best practices for delivering and developing training evaluations to maximize the benefits of leveraging emerging technologies?

992. How was the determination made for which training platforms would be used (i.e., media selection)?

993. To what degree are the teams goals and objectives clear, simple, and measurable?

994. Does adaptive training work?

995. To what extent are systems and applications (e.g., game engine, mobile device platform) utilized?

996. Does platform-specific assessment information contribute to training placement or tailoring of instruction (e.g. aptitude-treatment interaction)?

997. In what areas would you like to concentrate your knowledge and resources?

998. Does the rater (supervisor) have to wait for the interim or final performance assessment review to

tell an employee that the employees performance is unsatisfactory?

999. How should adaptive assessments be implemented?

1000. What are the standards or expectations for success?

1001. What is the Business Management Oversight Process?

1002. What innovations (if any) are developed to realize goals?

1003. Does statute or regulation require the job responsibility?

1004. What happens if a team member receives a Rating of Unsatisfactory?

1005. What is used as a basis for instructional decisions?

3.10 Issue Log: Predictive Analytics

1006. Are there common objectives between the team and the stakeholder?

1007. How often do you engage with stakeholders?

1008. What are the stakeholders interrelationships?

1009. What does the stakeholder need from the team?

1010. What is the impact on the risks?

1011. Who do you turn to if you have questions?

1012. What effort will a change need?

1013. Are they needed?

1014. Do you have members of your team responsible for certain stakeholders?

1015. Is the issue log kept in a safe place?

1016. Are the Predictive Analytics project issues uniquely identified, including to which product they refer?

1017. Persistence; will users learn a work around or will they be bothered every time?

1018. Why not more evaluators?

1019. What is a change?

1020. Are stakeholder roles recognized by your organization?

4.0 Monitoring and Controlling Process Group: Predictive Analytics

1021. Overall, how does the program function to serve the clients?

1022. How was the program set-up initiated?

1023. What areas were overlooked on this Predictive Analytics project?

1024. How will staff learn how to use the deliverables?

1025. How can you monitor progress?

1026. What is the timeline?

1027. What resources are necessary?

1028. Is progress on outcomes due to your program?

1029. Key stakeholders to work with. How many potential communications channels exist on the Predictive Analytics project?

1030. Contingency planning. if a risk event occurs, what will you do?

1031. Did the Predictive Analytics project team have enough people to execute the Predictive Analytics project plan?

1032. When will the Predictive Analytics project be

done?

1033. Have operating capacities been created and/or reinforced in partners?

1034. How well did the chosen processes fit the needs of the Predictive Analytics project?

1035. Who needs to be engaged upfront to ensure use of results?

4.1 Project Performance Report: Predictive Analytics

1036. What is the degree to which rules govern information exchange between individuals within your organization?

1037. To what degree can team members meet frequently enough to accomplish the teams ends?

1038. To what degree does the information network provide individuals with the information they require?

1039. To what degree does the funding match the requirement?

1040. To what degree do the structures of the formal organization motivate taskrelevant behavior and facilitate task completion?

1041. Next Steps?

1042. To what degree are the demands of the task compatible with and converge with the mission and functions of the formal organization?

1043. To what degree do team members feel that the purpose of the team is important, if not exciting?

1044. To what degree will the team adopt a concrete, clearly understood, and agreed-upon approach that will result in achievement of the teams goals?

1045. What degree are the relative importance and priority of the goals clear to all team members?

1046. To what degree are the tasks requirements reflected in the flow and storage of information?

1047. How is the data used?

1048. To what degree are sub-teams possible or necessary?

1049. How can Predictive Analytics project sustainability be maintained?

1050. To what degree does the formal organization make use of individual resources and meet individual needs?

4.2 Variance Analysis: Predictive Analytics

1051. Do you identify potential or actual budget-based and time-based schedule variances?

1052. Are all authorized tasks assigned to identified organizational elements?

1053. Are the wbs and organizational levels for application of the Predictive Analytics projected overhead costs identified?

1054. Who is generally responsible for monitoring and taking action on variances?

1055. What is your organizations rationale for sharing expenses and services between business segments?

1056. Is data disseminated to the contractors management timely, accurate, and usable?

1057. Are estimates of costs at completion generated in a rational, consistent manner?

1058. Are there knowledgeable Predictive Analytics projections of future performance?

1059. How does your organization allocate the cost of shared expenses and services?

1060. Who are responsible for the establishment of budgets and assignment of resources for overhead performance?

1061. Is there a logical explanation for any variance?

1062. Is cost and schedule performance measurement done in a consistent, systematic manner?

1063. Did an existing competitor change strategy?

1064. How do you evaluate the impact of schedule changes, work around, et?

1065. Did your organization lose existing customers and/or gain new customers?

1066. Are overhead cost budgets established for each department which has authority to incur overhead costs?

1067. What are the actual costs to date?

1068. Does the scheduling system identify in a timely manner the status of work?

4.3 Earned Value Status: Predictive Analytics

1069. How much is it going to cost by the finish?

1070. Are you hitting your Predictive Analytics projects targets?

1071. What is the unit of forecast value?

1072. Where are your problem areas?

1073. Verification is a process of ensuring that the developed system satisfies the stakeholders agreements and specifications; Are you building the product right? What do you haverify?

1074. If earned value management (EVM) is so good in determining the true status of a Predictive Analytics project and Predictive Analytics project its completion, why is it that hardly any one uses it in information systems related Predictive Analytics projects?

1075. When is it going to finish?

1076. Validation is a process of ensuring that the developed system will actually achieve the stakeholders desired outcomes; Are you building the right product? What do you validate?

1077. Earned value can be used in almost any Predictive Analytics project situation and in almost any Predictive Analytics project environment. it may be used on large Predictive Analytics projects, medium sized Predictive Analytics projects, tiny Predictive Analytics projects (in cut-down form), complex and simple Predictive Analytics projects and in any market sector. some people, of course, know all about earned value, they have used it for years - but perhaps not as effectively as they could have?

1078. Where is evidence-based earned value in your organization reported?

1079. How does this compare with other Predictive Analytics projects?

4.4 Risk Audit: Predictive Analytics

1080. The halo effect in business risk audits: can strategic risk assessment bias auditor judgment about accounting details?

1081. Is there (or should there be) some impact on the process of setting materiality when the auditor more effectively identifies higher risk areas of the financial statements?

1082. Is a software Predictive Analytics project management tool available?

1083. Do you have a realistic budget and do you present regular financial reports that identify how you are going against that budget?

1084. Are the software tools integrated with each other?

1085. What are the legal implications of not identifying a complete universe of business risks?

1086. Does the implementation method matter?

1087. Tradeoff: how much risk can be tolerated and still deliver the products where they need to be?

1088. What effect would a better risk management program have had?

1089. Are there any forms the staff is required to sign?

1090. Is the auditor truly independent?

1091. To what extent are auditors influenced by the business risk assessment in the audit process, and how can auditors create more effective mental models to more fully examine contradictory evidence?

1092. To what extent are auditors effective at linking business risks and management assertions?

1093. Can assurance be expanded beyond the traditional audit without undermining independence?

1094. What are the outcomes you are looking for?

1095. Is the auditor able to evaluate contradictory evidence in an unbiased manner?

1096. Do your financial policies and procedures ensure that each step in financial handling (receipt, recording, banking, reporting) is not completed by one person?

1097. How do you compare to other jurisdictions when managing the risk of ....?

1098. Do you have financial policies and procedures in place to guide officers of your organization/treasurer/general members?

4.5 Contractor Status Report: Predictive Analytics

1099. What process manages the contracts?

1100. What was the final actual cost?

1101. What was the budget or estimated cost for your organizations services?

1102. What was the actual budget or estimated cost for your organizations services?

1103. Describe how often regular updates are made to the proposed solution. Are corresponding regular updates included in the standard maintenance plan?

1104. If applicable; describe your standard schedule for new software version releases. Are new software version releases included in the standard maintenance plan?

1105. Are there contractual transfer concerns?

1106. How does the proposed individual meet each requirement?

1107. Who can list a Predictive Analytics project as organization experience, your organization or a previous employee of your organization?

1108. What are the minimum and optimal bandwidth requirements for the proposed soluiton?

1109. How is risk transferred?

1110. How long have you been using the services?

1111. What was the overall budget or estimated cost?

1112. What is the average response time for answering a support call?

4.6 Formal Acceptance: Predictive Analytics

1113. What is the Acceptance Management Process?

1114. Was the client satisfied with the Predictive Analytics project results?

1115. Do you buy pre-configured systems or build your own configuration?

1116. Who would use it?

1117. What was done right?

1118. Have all comments been addressed?

1119. Was the Predictive Analytics project goal achieved?

1120. What features, practices, and processes proved to be strengths or weaknesses?

1121. What lessons were learned about your Predictive Analytics project management methodology?

1122. Do you buy-in installation services?

1123. What function(s) does it fill or meet?

1124. Was the sponsor/customer satisfied?

1125. General estimate of the costs and times to complete the Predictive Analytics project?

1126. How well did the team follow the methodology?

1127. Did the Predictive Analytics project achieve its MOV?

1128. Was the Predictive Analytics project work done on time, within budget, and according to specification?

1129. What are the requirements against which to test, Who will execute?

1130. Does it do what client said it would?

1131. How does your team plan to obtain formal acceptance on your Predictive Analytics project?

1132. Is formal acceptance of the Predictive Analytics project product documented and distributed?

5.0 Closing Process Group: Predictive Analytics

1133. Is there a clear cause and effect between the activity and the lesson learned?

1134. What can you do better next time, and what specific actions can you take to improve?

1135. Are there funding or time constraints?

1136. When will the Predictive Analytics project be done?

1137. Did the Predictive Analytics project team have the right skills?

1138. Just how important is your work to the overall success of the Predictive Analytics project?

1139. Were sponsors and decision makers available when needed outside regularly scheduled meetings?

1140. Will the Predictive Analytics project deliverable(s) replace a current asset or group of assets?

1141. Does the close educate others to improve performance?

1142. What is the risk of failure to your organization?

1143. What was learned?

1144. What is the overall risk of the Predictive Analytics project to your organization?

1145. Were the outcomes different from the already stated planned?

1146. What is the Predictive Analytics project Management Process?

1147. Did the Predictive Analytics project team have enough people to execute the Predictive Analytics project plan?

5.1 Procurement Audit: Predictive Analytics

1148. Are behaviour modification applied to change procurement of goods and services if procurement is not functioning properly?

1149. Does the department have a procurement strategy and is it implemented?

1150. Was the submission of variant tenders accepted and duly ruled?

1151. Were products/services not received within the prescribed time limit?

1152. Is the purchase order form clear and complete so that the vendor understands all terms and conditions?

1153. Did the contracting authority offer unrestricted and full electronic access to the contract documents and any supplementary documents (specifying the internet address in the notice)?

1154. When performance conditions were detailed in the tender documentation, did the contracting authority verify if the tenders received met the already stated requirements?

1155. Was there a sound basis for the scorings applied to the criteria and was the scoring well balanced?

1156. Did you consider and evaluate alternatives, like bundling needs with other departments or grouping supplies in separate lots with different characteristics?

1157. Is each copy of the purchase order necessary?

1158. Were the documents received scrutinised for completion and adherence to stated conditions before the tenders were evaluated?

1159. Is there no evidence of unauthorized release of information or seemingly unnecessary contacts with bidders personnel during the evaluation and negotiation processes?

1160. Are there mechanisms in place to evaluate the performance of the departments suppliers?

1161. Who is verifying the performance of the contract and approving payments?

1162. Was the outcome of the award process properly reached and communicated?

1163. Are order quantities, deliveries and payment levels under the contract monitored by an appropriate official?

1164. Are outsourcing and Public Private Partnerships considered as alternatives to in-house work?

1165. How do you deal with budget constrains and assurance needs?

1166. Was the award criteria that of the most economically advantageous tender?

1167. Where required, were candidates registered as approved contractors, suppliers or service providers or certified by relevant bodies?

5.2 Contract Close-Out: Predictive Analytics

1168. Was the contract sufficiently clear so as not to result in numerous disputes and misunderstandings?

1169. Was the contract complete without requiring numerous changes and revisions?

1170. How is the contracting office notified of the automatic contract close-out?

1171. Change in circumstances?

1172. Has each contract been audited to verify acceptance and delivery?

1173. Change in attitude or behavior?

1174. What happens to the recipient of services?

1175. Parties: Authorized?

1176. Change in knowledge?

1177. What is capture management?

1178. Have all contracts been closed?

1179. Have all contract records been included in the Predictive Analytics project archives?

1180. Was the contract type appropriate?

1181. Have all acceptance criteria been met prior to final payment to contractors?

1182. How does it work?

1183. How/when used ?

1184. Parties: who is involved?

1185. Have all contracts been completed?

1186. Are the signers the authorized officials?

5.3 Project or Phase Close-Out: Predictive Analytics

1187. In preparing the Lessons Learned report, should it reflect a consensus viewpoint, or should the report reflect the different individual viewpoints?

1188. What were the desired outcomes?

1189. Which changes might a stakeholder be required to make as a result of the Predictive Analytics project?

1190. Did the delivered product meet the specified requirements and goals of the Predictive Analytics project?

1191. Complete yes or no?

1192. Did the Predictive Analytics project management methodology work?

1193. Planned remaining costs?

1194. Who controlled key decisions that were made?

1195. Who is responsible for award close-out?

1196. What benefits or impacts does the stakeholder group expect to obtain as a result of the Predictive Analytics project?

1197. Planned completion date?

1198. Were cost budgets met?

1199. How often did each stakeholder need an update?

1200. What are they?

1201. What information did each stakeholder need to contribute to the Predictive Analytics projects success?

1202. What is this stakeholder expecting?

1203. Was the schedule met?

1204. Who exerted influence that has positively affected or negatively impacted the Predictive Analytics project?

1205. Is the lesson significant, valid, and applicable?

1206. What were the actual outcomes?

5.4 Lessons Learned: Predictive Analytics

1207. Were the Predictive Analytics project goals attained?

1208. How many government and contractor personnel are authorized for the Predictive Analytics project?

1209. Who needs to learn lessons?

1210. How clear were you on your role in the Predictive Analytics project?

1211. How well were your expectations met regarding the extent of your involvement in the Predictive Analytics project (effort, time commitments, etc.)?

1212. Was the purpose of the Predictive Analytics project, the end products and success criteria clearly defined and agreed at the start?

1213. Did the Predictive Analytics project improve the team members reputations, skills, personal development?

1214. How objective was the collection of data?

1215. How well did the Predictive Analytics project Manager respond to questions or comments related to the Predictive Analytics project?

1216. Did the Predictive Analytics project change significantly?

1217. How well were expectations met regarding the frequency and content of information that was conveyed to by the Predictive Analytics project Manager?

1218. How effective were the techniques used to prepare you and your organization for the impact of the changes brought about by the product or service produced by the Predictive Analytics project?

1219. Was the user/client satisfied with the end product?

1220. Were quality procedures built into the Predictive Analytics project?

1221. What were the lessons learned on this Predictive Analytics project?

1222. What regulatory regime controlled how your organization head and program manager directed your organization and Predictive Analytics project?

1223. What were the problems encountered in the Predictive Analytics project-functional area relationship, why, and how could they be fixed?

1224. What things surprised you on the Predictive Analytics project that were not in the plan?

1225. What is the proportion of in-house and contractor personnel authorized for the Predictive Analytics project?

1226. How useful was the content of the training you received in preparation for the use of the product/ service?

Index

clearly 12, 17, 21, 26, 28, 31, 33, 40, 56, 71, 73, 83, 95, 139, 149, 187, 235, 256
client   8, 11, 41, 115, 133, 196, 200, 245-246, 257
clients 28, 233
closed 84, 203, 206, 217, 252
closely 11
Close-Out   6, 204, 252, 254
closest 111
Closing6, 60, 247
Coaches   29, 32, 183
coalitions   129
Cognitive   43
cognizant   228
coherent   202
colleague   104
colleagues   104, 107, 166
collect 54, 85, 174, 182, 227
collected   34-35, 41, 48, 57, 60, 79
collection   41-42, 44, 51, 54, 62, 64, 182, 256
combining   60
coming   61
command   89, 196
comments   245, 256
commercial   149
commit   193, 207
commitment 86, 116
committed   35, 111, 146, 152, 171, 189, 192, 202
committee   204, 215
common   172, 204, 231
community   166, 174-175, 201
companies   1, 8, 87, 218
company   7, 51, 67, 98, 103-104, 112, 115-116, 118
compare   57, 78, 240, 242
compared   117, 189, 197-198
comparing   75
comparison   12
compatible   206, 216, 235
compelling   30
competitor   130, 238
complain   181
complaint   220
complaints   220

impact 4-5, 31-32, 43, 47-48, 51, 53-54, 72, 111, 125, 137, 165, 173, 176, 184, 194-196, 198, 211, 216-217, 224, 227, 231, 238, 241, 257

impacted 146, 255

impacting 43

impacts 145, 166, 194, 254

implement 18, 47, 62, 83

implicit 98

importance 204, 227, 236

important 23, 45, 57, 66, 96, 98, 102, 106, 108, 115, 117, 132, 163, 165, 180, 190, 208, 228, 235, 247

improve 2, 11-12, 49, 69, 71, 73-75, 77, 79-81, 162, 179, 223, 247, 256

improved 72, 74, 77-79, 93, 129

improving 80, 213

inaccurate 138

incentives 91

incident 219

include 77, 154, 164, 205, 227

included 2, 9, 69, 143, 175, 199, 243, 252

includes 10, 44, 208

including 22, 28-29, 46, 63, 76, 85, 87, 146, 220, 231

inclusion 220

incoming 65

incomplete 138

increase 79, 116

increased 109

increasing 109, 219

incurring 149, 185

in-depth 9, 12

indicate 46, 92, 105, 111

indicated 88

indicators 44-45, 47, 57, 59, 66, 73, 150

indirect 149, 185

indirectly 1

individual 1, 19, 41, 61, 131, 167-168, 184, 186, 225, 228, 236, 243, 254

industry 88, 107, 117, 135, 158, 171, 189, 202, 220

infinite 103

influence 74, 108, 128, 132, 191, 203, 218-219, 255

influenced 242

influences 129, 158

inform 68

preventive 200
prevents 23
previous 31, 169, 243
previously 192, 216
pricing 41
primarily 189
printing 8
priorities 42, 45
priority 236
Privacy 59
Private 250
probably 162
problem 17-18, 21, 23-26, 28, 31, 34-35, 45, 59, 66-67, 136, 139-140, 212, 218, 239
problems 19, 22-24, 43, 66, 76-78, 88, 97, 204, 257
procedure 164, 215, 220-221, 225
procedures 11, 85, 88, 92, 136, 149, 151-152, 161, 169, 178, 180, 182, 214, 242, 257
proceeding 167
process 1-7, 11, 27, 30-33, 35, 41, 43-44, 46, 49, 52-53, 57-58, 60-67, 73-75, 78, 83-85, 87, 89, 92-93, 124, 131-132, 134-138, 141, 143-146, 152, 161, 165, 172, 177, 179, 182-183, 192-193, 206, 208, 210, 214, 219, 222, 224, 227-228, 230, 233, 239, 241-243, 245, 247-248, 250
processes 37, 49, 52, 59-64, 67, 69, 87, 91, 125, 132, 135, 146, 151, 189, 192-193, 216, 220, 234, 245, 250
processing 87
produce 125, 161, 212, 223
produced 53, 81, 257
produces 155
producing 141, 143
product 1, 11, 54, 57, 66, 121, 138, 158, 176, 192, 196, 211-212, 216, 223, 231, 239, 246, 254, 257-258
production 109
productive 185
products 1, 20, 22, 51, 107, 114, 138, 141, 210, 213, 216, 241, 249, 256
program 24, 93, 107, 132, 173, 186, 233, 241, 257
programmed 99
Programs 212
progress 27, 53, 79, 85, 119-120, 126, 130-131, 144, 174, 179, 183, 189, 210, 233

remedial 52
remedies 46
remove 68, 82, 200
remunerate 118
repeatable 57
rephrased 11
replace 247
replaced 132
replanning 150
report 5-6, 54, 90, 204, 212, 220, 223, 235, 243, 254
reported 202, 204, 240
reporting 91, 138, 149, 165, 192, 214, 242
reports 45, 86, 128, 138, 184, 241
repository 60, 170, 203
represent 74, 216
reproduced 1
reputation 102
request 5, 67, 138, 214, 216-217
requested 1, 77, 216
requests 214
require 48, 92, 161, 192, 195, 230, 235
required 22, 24, 31, 36, 39, 56, 68, 73, 80, 88, 125, 135, 138,
150, 153, 155, 166, 168, 185, 198, 208-209, 241, 251, 254
requiring 128, 252
research 18, 119, 144, 221, 229
resemble 211
reserved 1
reserves 184
reside 172
resolution 63, 226
resolve 24, 155, 223
resolved 203, 226
resource 3-4, 113, 131, 135, 155, 161-163, 170, 188, 212
resources 2, 9, 18, 20, 27, 36, 38, 41, 49, 52, 73, 76, 86, 88-
89, 103, 107, 113, 139, 143, 153, 155, 162, 165, 174, 220, 223, 229,
233, 236-237
respect 1
respond 131, 225, 256
responded 13
responding 194
response 18, 24, 84, 87-88, 91-92, 165, 244
responses 117, 204
responsive 166, 175

Lightning Source UK Ltd.
Milton Keynes UK
UKHW020728050119
335015UK00011B/537/P